MANY MINDS

MANY MINDS

Critical Essays on American Writers

CARL VAN DOREN

KENNIKAT PRESS, INC./PORT WASHINGTON, N. Y.

MANY MINDS

Copyright 1924 by Alfred A. Knopf, Inc.
This edition reissued by Kennikat Press in 1966

Library of Congress Catalog Card No: 66-21389

Indexed in the ESSAY & GENERAL LITERATURE INDEX

TO
W. P. TRENT

CONTENTS

CONTENTS

I. SUBSOIL

THE AMERICAN RHYTHM

Mary Austin

THE cultures of an older world come to America as pioneers cross the mountains and the prairies: they leave behind them, that is, many possessions which seemed too heavy to be carried along and many which were light enough to be overlooked. But when they have established themselves in the new region they begin to miss most of the things they could or did not bring and if they prosper they undertake to create them or to import them. Creation and importation henceforth run a perennial race. For the most part, the necessities have been invented and made at home, the luxuries brought in from lands more ancient and more adroit. From England have come the modes of play and sport, from Germany scholarship and music, from France painting and sculpture and fashions in dress. The arts, with philosophy, have thus in the United States rarely been quite indigenous.

Something of Europe or Asia clings to them.
Nor does this mean merely that the forms of art,
such as the Greek temple, the oratorio, the sonnet, the nude statue, the learned monograph, are
here employed without great variation from their
alien originals; it means also that the ways of
looking at life and the methods of expressing the
significance of it in some durable idiom are af-
fected by the alien language in which the artist
ordinarily speaks. It is as if a man should
make love in a tongue not wholly native to him
and so should be betrayed into seeming less passionate, less direct, less convincing than if he
spoke in words which not only had been on his
lips from infancy but which had also through
previous generations been ingrained in the stuff
of his being. As a consequence much of the
finest American thought and feeling has been ut-
tered in a dialect which is almost mandarin in
its remoteness from the customary speech of the
nation; and the vernacular in philosophy, archi-
tecture, literature, and the fine arts has busied
itself with minor concerns or at least with concerns which have been so little regarded that they
have grown up with little discipline or guidance.
Sound speculative treatises go unread while the
wisdom of the people shapes itself into rough

popular humor; serious builders worry over respectable cathedrals while office buildings thrust their heads into the sky with an unattended beauty; between academic odes and Negro folksongs there is a hollow chasm. No small part of the strength of innovators has been spent in trying to bridge this chasm. Yet the best William James, for instance, could do was to shape a more or less coherent logic for the American gospel of workability; the best Walt Whitman could do was to graft the dithyramb upon the stump speech; the best Edward MacDowell could do was to weld Indian themes into a symphony. Somewhere back of these divergences is there not some common ground for the American philosopher or artist to stand upon?

2

The work of Mary Austin had been to discover that common ground and to prophesy its uses. Born in the Middle West, now apparently the center of the nation's greatest energy, she lived her maturing years in a kind of desert isolation in California. There she had her vision, there she found what she felt to be her place in the cosmic scheme. "For all the toll the desert takes of a man," she wrote in her first book, "it gives compensations, deep breaths, deep sleep, and the communion of the stars. It comes upon one with new force in the pauses of the night that the Chaldeans were a desert-bred people. It is hard to escape the sense of mastery as the stars move in the wide clear heavens to risings and settings unobscured. They look large and near and palpitant; as if they moved on some stately service not needful to declare. Wheeling to their stations in the sky, they make the poor world-fret of no account. Of no account you who lie out there watching, nor the lean coyote that stands off in the scrub from you and howls and howls."

During this period in the desert, too, Mrs. Austin arrived at her conceptions of those human matters which have interested her: religion, art, love, character, society. In that simple universe, where she came to seem a kind of prophetess to the simple people who lived around her, she watched the procession of birth, love, hate, aspiration, death, and the marching seasons. The first philosophers she knew were silent men innocent of sophistication; the first poets she knew were Indians whose songs had in them nothing of the divided art of white America. She endured hardships, she tasted immense bitterness, she healed herself with thought. The mark of the desert has never quite left her. It appears in the profound calm of her temper, in the large dimensions of her ideas, in her neglect of all that does not go to the roots of some matter or other, in her oracular habit of communication. Interpreting the desert to a more complicated world, she interprets that world to itself. By the desert she takes her measure of existence.

And yet, unlike most American writers with some chosen province from which to scan the others, Mrs. Austin has steadily refused to settle down and wear out her material by exploiting it. When, twenty years ago, she published *The Land of Little Rain* an older mood of romance was warring with the new mood of naturalism. Yielding herself to neither, she in a sense laid hold on both. Rich as the magic was with which she invested that dry land, she looked at it with singularly level eyes, relying upon history and science in her account and celebrating the human nature of the desert with an eloquence which somehow managed to be analytical. But though she won a prompt success with her report of the locality which she had discovered for literature, she seems seldom to have been tempted to repeat herself. Each new book has been notably unlike its predecessor. For this reason, if for no other, she has lacked the particular kind of reputation which is won by a continued strumming upon one note. Even if she had wanted to, she could probably never have achieved a strategic monotony. What she has written has been essentially the record of her growth, the growth of a deep and powerful spirit which has lived by extending its inquiries and its experiences. If now and then during her career she has found her record, as written in her books and delivered in her speeches, becoming less generally listened to than at other times, she has done little about it but has gone confidently on. "Once in every seven years," she says, "New York discovers me." There is something characteristic in the amused egotism of her remark; there is something significant in the fact at which she hints. After all she has lived her life as close to the ground-swell of the nation as she could get. No wonder that it should, by some rhythmic rise and fall, bring her occasionally to the surface of the national consciousness and then let her sink back again during another quiet interval.

Though the range of her concerns has been great, they fall under a few large heads. She has studied landscape and climate, with their human consequences, in *The Land of Little*

Rain, The Flock, and *Lost Borders.* She has studied the plight of genius, of the individual by some gift made incapable of conformity to an environment, in *A Woman of Genius, The Arrow-Maker, The Man Jesus.* She has specifically studied the nature of love in *Love and the Soul-Maker,* the position of women in *The Young Woman Citizen,* the basis of national art in *The American Rhythm.* She has made herself an expert, for all practical literary purposes, in Amerindian lore, and has in countless papers and addresses turned her grave scrutiny upon religion, sex, ethics, communal life, handicrafts, history, anthropology. In none of her concerns, however, is she far removed from any other. Her conception of landscape and climate touches all she writes. *A Woman of Genius* and *The Arrow-Maker* are, though works of art, none the less documents upon the struggle of women to lead, like men, lives not wholly circumscribed by their biological functions. The Jesus of her interpretation is a genius, taught by the desert, who goes to his mission and his fate among the people of towns who destroy him because his reverence to them seems blasphemy, so far are they strangers to habits of direct vision such as his. All that Mrs. Austin writes is interwoven, for

[9]

she has, it appears, no tight compartments in her mind. The whole stream of her experience and reflection has passed through her and, no matter what the theme at any moment, has taken the color of her spirit.

3

Her eminence arises from the abundance of that spirit. No one can estimate it properly who has not heard her speak. Some hearers she alienates by a forthright and unblinking candor which cannot be called by any milder term than egotism; some by the occasional looseness of her technical knowledge and the bold hand with which she uses it to draw bold general conclusions; some by the irony which is virtually her only form of humor. Yet these are but outward qualities. Those of her hearers who can disregard them find themselves listening to words which have the authority of something curiously first-hand. She speaks as if she had just come back from the desert with fresh truth. But the desert from which she has come is not in California; it is in the clear country of the mind. The temptation is to say that the region lies deeper: in the soul, perhaps, or in the memory of the race. Yet a hearer who is chary of such terms may still admit that as she speaks he finds himself responding out of deeps in his own spirit. As if she were a sybil in a cave, he is aware of profound vibrations accompanying her voice. From every sentence rings of thought are thrown off, widening out till they are lost again beyond the reach of common speculation.

Yet, as with all oracles, it will not do to examine the spell of such a moment too crabbedly, or to try to repeat in ordinary prose what Mrs. Austin has just said. Other mystics have had most of her revelations, and not one of them has ever been able to prove to a really courageous or to a merely flippant skeptic that a given revelation must be trusted. This All into which they testify to having felt that they were merged— it is as much an hypothesis as an experience. So too with the stream of life which mystics feel when they turn to more purely human matters. Is it actually a kind of river on which the millions of individual beings are borne from birth to death, and perhaps to other births and other deaths; or is it merely a stupendous array of parallel lines, a line to a life, no one touching another, without the interfusions and cohesions which are ordinarily assumed? Nothing in human knowledge can answer such a question overwhelmingly. Mrs. Austin, however, starts with the primary assumptions of a God, or Allness, and of a life-stream, and she sees all existence under the light of these assumptions. Doubt them, or fail to feel them, and you may wonder that she should be so impressive as she is. It is at this point that she comes into conflict with the brasher intellectuals, who will not share her long views. To such of her critics she seems solemn if not pompous; to her they seem thin and ephemeral intelligences playing with fragmentary toys. Rarely enough have prophets spoken the language of the people they came to serve.

As a prophet, however, Mrs. Austin must be judged. She stands in this respect even the vulgar test of being asked which of her prophecies have come true. A decade before the newer forms of verse came into fashion, she had forecast them and practised them, deriving her methods from those of the primitive Americans near whom she lived. Her interpretations of various movements of opinion and sentiment about religion, the status of women, the forms of society, have been delivered in instance after instance so early as to have, apparently, an element of prophecy in them. And in the less vulgar aspects of her calling she has always had

more than a little, and often much, of the seer's
technic. Without it she could never have cut, as
she has cut, through the surface of appearances to
the reality beneath. Thanks to the long views
which she takes, and which are the best signs
of a prophet, she has not fallen fatally into any
mere habits of thought or feeling. Over that
stream of life upon which she incessantly broods,
she sees that thickening crusts of habit are forever being formed. Prophets and men of science
have from time to time detected, or thought they
detected, some tendency, some pattern in the
stream. Once accepted, these guesses have been
turned by the common faith into substantial dog-
mas, able to survive long after the tendency has
veered, the pattern shifted by reason of new cir-
cumstances. Then, Mrs. Austin knows, it is for
new prophets and men of science to announce
new guesses, even though they thereby risk the
club, the stake, excommunication, exile. That
she is of the breed of prophets should appear, to
contemporaries who cannot measure her by the
test of fulfillment, from her preoccupation with
the changing current. Let any dogmatist stand
where he will upon whatever stiff crust of prejudice, and if he talks with Mrs. Austin he will
catch some sound of the stream stirring beneath

his feet. Let him watch her career, and he will see how often she has been one of the first to point out that here or there the pattern was breaking up.

4

Any discussion of Mrs. Austin's achievement tends irresistibly to turn rather to her prophecy than to her art, as it tends to turn rather to her whole intentions than to her specific triumphs. No one of her books more than partially represents her. Her verse, for example, sounds slight by comparison with her searching plea for a native poetry that shall not content itself with the deft adaptation of this or that imported, sophisticated mode, but shall go down within the nation till it reaches the basic rhythms, the stroke of the paddle·or of the ax, the curves of the landscape, the sequence of the weather and the crops. This indeed she admits: "mine," she says, "is not a singing gift." Nor does she succeed entirely in more dramatic undertakings. *The Arrow-Maker* has a theme to which Mrs. Austin has given as much thought and passion as to any other among the many which have engaged her: the conflict in a woman between the special endowment which parts her from her kind and the universal instinct which draws her back to the customary life of love and child-bearing. The setting of the play, among the Indians of the Southwest, is one of which Mrs. Austin has a masterly knowledge, as she has also of the tribal customs which give color to the action. Yet as a drama *The Arrow-Maker* does less than justice to theme or setting. Except for a few splendid moments, it does not move with the true, cruel rush of tragedy; though the language is high and pure, it lacks something of the authentic breath of human speech. On the whole Mrs. Austin is at her best when she is nearer to exposition or criticism than to invention or creation. To be explicit, she nowhere else quite equals the success she reaches in those lovely, luminous documents on the Southwest, *The Land of Little Rain, The Flock, Lost Borders,* and the forthcoming volume in which she will return to that territory, *The Land of Journeys' Ending.* To put it very broadly, she is much less than herself unless both her knowledge and her passion are in something like equipoise.

What talent is it that is withheld from a writer like Mrs. Austin and is given to a writer like, say, H. G. Wells, who neither knows as much nor feels as profoundly as she does, yet who has twice the capacity for pouring himself into effective forms of art? Perhaps it is the talent for strategic ignorance, which she lacks as well as strategic monotony. Men and Wellses have the advantage over angels and Mrs. Austins that they rush in unafraid, no matter what the peril. Art, after all, is action, not reflection. The artist must strike, must put himself behind the blow, without too much weighing of the consequences, whether to himself or to abstract truth. Let it not appear that Mrs. Austin is always accurate or ever timid. But she has a spacious mind, with many inlets. Within it she revolves and broods, turning over all the sciences, building up huge structures of doctrine, constantly shaping the universe in reasonable forms. Then when she comes to utter what has taken shape within her, she hesitates. Or if she does not consciously hesitate, she is nevertheless held back by the weight of her speculations. So much as she has assembled cannot crowd with impetuous haste through the outlet of her art. Perhaps, however, it is wiser not to give much credit to ignorance, strategic or otherwise. It may be that what Mrs. Austin lacks is the ability to focus her diffused powers and interests, however great, within a necessarily narrow field. The far-sighted sometimes fumble when they try to do neat tasks near at hand.

OLD WISDOM IN A NEW TONGUE

George Ade

IF Samos, or whatever Grecian neighborhood it was, had its Æsop, so has Indiana its George Ade. His business is to give flesh and blood to maxims. Making maxims is next to the oldest business in the world. As soon as any creature has learned an art or trick which helps him to prosper in his affairs, he sets out to tell others how they too may prosper; and the sum of such advice is wisdom. Fish in their wet caves, one may imagine, concisely counsel their offspring what banks to hunt along and what glittering baits to shun. Birds teach their fledglings how to spread their new wings at a proper angle, how to be architects of nests, how to observe a happy economy with regard to worms and beetles. Bees propound the advantages of buckwheat over clover or of honeysuckle over morning-glories and tell how stings may be planted with the most desirable consequences. Bears, while they are licking their cubs into proper shape, growl neat secrets into their ears about the taste of roots and nuts and about the nicer points of successful hibernation. Though such biology is rather picturesque than trustworthy, it serves to hint at the long antiquity of human wisdom, which comes down from a time earlier than literature and virtually as early as speech itself. Cavemen, squatting safe behind the fire which kept out the sabertooth, doubtless invented or repeated guttural aphorisms for the benefit of their sons. The swart Egyptians working in their annual mud and the fair Sumerians setting up their towers of Babel gossiped in the evenings, it is reasonably certain, about the ways of life. So Æsop, when he made his fables, or Solomon, when he made his proverbs, had only to add his own wit to the wisdom of many other observers and philosophers.

2

Wisdom, it may be argued, is the same in all generations, but the idiom of wisdom varies. Since Solomon chose proverbs, and Æsop fables, most popular moralists have followed one or the other of these two. Among the older Yankees there was a Franklin who, knowing that most of them who were not shopkeepers were farmers, told the one group to "Keep thy shop, and thy shop will keep thee" and warned the other that "The rotten apple spoils his companions." Among the newer Hoosiers there is a George Ade who, intimately kin to the folk and yet detached from it by genius, puts his observations into moral tales such as *The New Fable of the Toilsome Ascent and the Shining Table-Land* and *The Fable of the Wise Piker Who Had the Kind of Talk That Went.* Between them lies a long tradition of vernacular philosophers: Jack Downing, Hosea Biglow, Josh Billings, Artemus Ward, Mark Twain, Mr. Dooley—each the continuer of the old wisdom and the inventor of a new idiom. George Ade, indeed, was so immersed in the tradition that he was slow in emerging as himself, with a form and dialect which fitted him as the garments of such a satirist should. However amusing his plays were, they were cast in molds which other dramatists had furnished him. Even such racy triumphs as his early stories about Artie and Pink Marsh and Doc Horne do not show Mr. Ade at his most distinctive. Only gradually did he hit upon his

[20]

natural device, perfect it, and settle down to working within its ample limits.

But though he had to hunt ten years for a form, he was very ready to use it when he found it. His mind was crowded with observations made on a plane which was intensely typical of the established American folk. He had been born and had grown up among the farms and villages of Indiana, tightest of the Mid-Western States; he had put on a larger cunning in Chicago, a village which had become a city too fast to lose its old traits at once; he was always bent on returning to the original neighborhood where he was most at home. In his almost simultaneous *Fables in Slang, More Fables, Forty Modern Fables,* and the later volumes which their quick success called for, he walked close to a fertile soil, along accepted folk-ways. What was first apparent in his work was an amused distrust of all who leave the beaten highway by any but the beaten by-paths. The parents of Joseph and Clarence are so fussy with the elder and so slack with the younger that both boys go wrong, having left the comfortable middle ground of ordinary custom. Lutie, who pesters the village with her voice, imagines she is a great singer until she submits herself to the test of the box-office and an impartial critic; the Coming Champion, likewise, passes for a whirlwind until he puts on the gloves with a real pugilist, who blithely knocks the youngster out and sends him back, humbled, to a safer occupation. Handsome Jethro, who scorns rough work, manages in ten years to save up nineteen dollars of his salary in a five-and-ten-cent store, while his brother Lyford in that same time buys and stocks a valuable farm. The magnate who in his youth aspired to be a congressman barely misses apoplexy when, at the peak of his success, he comes upon his high-school oration and remembers that he once urged "all young Patriots to leap into the Arena and with the Shield of Virtue quench the rising Flood of Corruption." The Benevolent Lady who looks through a lorgnette into the case of the poor discovers that they regard her attentions as an insult, and returns, though in a huff, to concerns which are less philanthropic.

3

To put it briefly, the central moral of George Ade's fables is that those get along best who best mind their own business. But these fables are less simple in their application than the maxims, say, of Franklin. Assuming no less than Franklin the merits of industry and economy and temperance and foresight, Mr. Ade knows that the times have changed. The folk he speaks for has heard the old prudential maxims so long that it has begun to note exceptions. One of his characters, a caddy, hurts his head trying to figure out why his hard-working father "could seldom get one Dollar to rub against another," while the golfers whom the boy sees forever playing "had Money to throw at the Birds." In another fable the brother who is the book-worm of a certain legal office does the drudgery and looks shabby while the brother who is the butterfly of the firm has the fun and gets the credit. In still another, Luella the busy, but homely, girl rises no further in the world than to the post of cook in the household of her lazy, but pretty, sister Mae. Perhaps, the fables keep hinting, honesty is not always the only policy. Perhaps it is true that "Early to Bed and Early to Rise and you will meet very few of our best people." Perhaps there is more topsyturvy in the moral world than the maxim-mongers have made out.

As a satirist of genius Mr. Ade goes, of course, beyond the folk in his perception of the ironies which attend prosperity, and yet he derives the body of his wit from a very general Hoosier wisdom. His fulcrum and his point of view are Hoosier. His people no less than he, whatever illusions they may cling to, have a steady suspicion of saints and poets and reformers, of snobbishness and eccentricity and affectation. Like him, they are tickled by tales of townsmen who come off second best in bargains with rustics or with villagers; of rude Westerners who do not suffer by comparison with Easterners of a higher polish; of simple Americans who, having tried the shining routes of Europe, come joyfully back to the familiar habits of their inland home. They like to laugh at windy statesmen, but are willing to smile at politicians who hoodwink the populace cleverly. They encourage aspiration, but they snicker at the mean arts by which mean persons seek to make themselves conspicuous in the world without real excellence. They look askance at rhetoric, at rebellion, at ecstasy. For the most part they confine their talk to the essential topics of work and play and love, but they will take none of these too seriously: they hold that work must have its interludes, that play must not degenerate into hard labor, and that love must be regarded, or at least discussed, as one of the aspects of comedy. Inveterately middle class

[24]

themselves, they feel for proletariats a contempt which is modified by democratic sentiment, and for aristocracies a contempt which is modified by a sneaking curiosity. Inveterately nativist themselves, they despise all foreigners and new-comers and do not pretend to understand them. At the same time they are sure enough of their position in a settled order to delight in jokes at their expense, or at the expense of their neighbors, provided the jokes are in their own language and are made by some one whose standing is established.

4

It is here that a personage like George Ade comes into the picture. He belongs so unquestionably to his folk that he has a license to ridicule it. Being a part of the country, he is himself a victim of any laughter which he may bring upon its inhabitants. Then, too, he knows its prejudices. He knows what types of folly are regularly mocked and what are not. He does not challenge any of the profounder doctrines; he only grins at shallow doctrinaires. He troubles no one by following the reason too far, into territory where it radically dissents from tne very bases of popular belief. And even when he goes beyond his public in his criticism of its accepted notions, he does it with such evidences of kind familiarity that his superiority is forgiven in the pleasures of recognition that he gives. He is minutely conversant with the ins and outs of common households; with the wiles of maidens and their swains; with the ways of men with dogs and horses and motors and stenographers and customers and competitors, in the bleachers, on the golf links, at the poker table; with the ways of women with servants and pets and clergymen and house-cleaning and candy and cosmetics, in cotillions, on picnics, at bargain counters; with all the comic nooks of average American life which may be looked into by an observer whose eyes have every sharpness except that which comes from passionate insight.

That Mr. Ade is primarily a moralist appears in his practice of seeing his characters all as types. Though they may have names and local habitations, they do not particularly need them; their being typical is what makes them significant. Yet he is too much an artist to be entirely satisfied with what is general. He multiplies concrete detail with an abundance rarely to be found in moralists. One of his best fables may serve to illustrate his method in all of them.

OLD WISDOM

The New Fable of Susan and the Daughter and the Grand-Daughter, and Then Something Really Grand is a comic history in little of American luxury. Susan, who was seventeen in Pennsylvania in 1840, married Rufus, and with him "decided to hit a New Trail into the Dark Timber and grow up with the Boundless West." In Illinois, when they had been settled a few years, Rufus once on a trip to the nearest town "thought of the brave Woman who was back there in the lonesome Shack, shooing the Prairie Wolves away from the Cradle, and he resolved to reward her. With only three Gills of Stone Fence under his Wammus he spread his Wild-Cat Currency on the Counter and purchased a $6 clock with jig-saw ornaments, a shiny coat of varnish, and a Bouquet of Pink Roses on the door." Jennie, their daughter, the fable proceeds, married Hiram, money-changer and merchant, and lived in the county seat. "Hiram was in rugged Health, having defended the flag by Proxy during the recent outcropping of Acrimony between the devotees of Cold Bread and the slaves of Hot Biscuit. . . . The fact that Jennie was his wife gave her quite a Standing with him. He admired her for having made such a Success of her Life." Once "while in

Chicago to buy his Winter Stock, he bargained for two days and finally bought a Cottage Melodeon, with the Stool thrown in." Their daughter Frances married a Chicago man named Willoughby who had inherited a part of State Street and spent his time watching the "Unearned Increment piling up on every Corner." Having filled their house with period furniture, Willoughby wanted to do more, and bought his wife a "rubber-tired Victoria, drawn by two expensive Bang-Tails in jingly Harness and surmounted by important Turks in overwhelming Livery." Therefore, in 1913, the daughter of Frances and Willoughby arrived in Reno and began proceedings for a divorce against her husband Hubert because he had refused to buy her an eighty-thousand-dollar necklace. The moral, the tale concludes, is that "Rufus had no business buying the clock."

In this humorous allegory of the clock and its consequences Mr. Ade moves through an expanding century, touching each of the generations with a sure, if hilarious, hand, using the most specific and most temporary illustrations and yet investing them all with a wide comic significance, playing the light of his observation everywhere and setting off the fireworks of his language in celebration of the absurdities he encounters. In the same fashion he moves through his own time. Very notably he possesses the courage to be characteristic of the folk which he represents in his fables. His hand might have been stayed by the desire to make his folk appear a little more intelligent, a little more witty, a little more decorous, a little more quaint and curious than it is. But Mr. Ade has the disposition as well as the knack of candor. If he is enough detached from his native country to be able to see across it, he is also close enough to it to feel no need for apologizing because it, like other native countries, is not different from what it is. He cuts the garment of his satire to fit the figure for which it is intended. That the figure is often angular and awkward he would not deny, but he would deny that it is his business to disguise it. Nor would he make any particular effort to correct it. Coming as he does with laughter, not with anger, to his job, serious but never impassioned, he yet takes a hearty pleasure in demolishing by his ridicule the reformers, climbers, Bohemians, zealous or shiftless souls of all denominations who secede from the homely circle of the average. To look into his vernacular fables for poetry, elevation, denunciation, tragedy, subtle

[29]

processes of the mind or the emotions is simply
to look for them in the wrong place, as it would
be to look for them in any of the ancient or modern fabulists. Mr. Ade's fables deal with the
visible ways of the tangible world in which the
vast majority of Americans live.

5

In no respect is he at once more representative
and yet more distinctive than in the dialect he
employs. He is representative because he has
that sixth sense for language which is one of the
marks of Americans. Like his compatriots of
various grades of learning, he revels, he rolls in
breath-taking metaphors, jolting surprises, swash-
buckling exaggerations. He is a voice for those
Americans who, generally without knowing it,
feel that their native tongue has suddenly been
released from the bondage of a stiff, formal
classicism, or rather, to put it more idiomatically,
has been turned out to grass and is scampering
around the pasture kicking up its heels. He is
distinctive because he outdoes a nation of slang-
makers at their own game. In part he relies
upon the mere trick of capitals for his effect; in
part he gathers racy phrases from many quarters
and fits them into astounding mosaic patterns.

But besides doing these relatively easy things, he also creates. "I have been working for years," he says with a broad and possibly not uncomplacent grin, "to enrich the English language. Most of the time I have been years ahead of the dictionaries. I have been so far ahead of the dictionaries that sometimes I fear they will never catch up." And yet it is not so much that he has invented actual words themselves as that he has invented new combinations, new short cuts. Thus he says that a certain man and wife and daughter were thriving: "The Fairy Wand had been waved above the snide Bungalow, and it was now a Queen Anne Château dripping with Dewdads of Scroll Work and congested with Black Walnut. The Goddess took her Mocha in the Feathers, and a Music Teacher came twice each week to bridge the awful chasm between Dorothy and Chopin. Dinner had been moved up to Milking Time." By only one word ("dewdads") is Mr. Ade here ahead of the best American dictionary; "took her Mocha in the Feathers" is obviously a native equivalent for "had her breakfast in bed"; but only George Ade would have hit upon this way of saying that the family now dined six or seven hours later than their agricultural forebears, or that Dorothy had

[31]

not been born with much gift for music. If it is the luck of Mr. Ade to have issued from a nation which breeds and encourages such verbal pyrotechnics, it is his own merit to have devised a dialect which mingles the rapture of surprise with the satisfaction of comprehensibility. One of the simplest tests of an ingrained American is to try whether in reading these fables he instantly understands even those locutions which he has never met before.

For outlanders it is different. "Andrew Lang," declares Mr. Ade, "once started to read my works and then sank with a bubbling cry and did not come up for three days." This suggests a question which should be noticed: Will posterity, at home or elsewhere, have any better fate than a transatlantic contemporary like Andrew Lang? The chances are, must be the answer to the question, that the dictionaries will never quite catch up. They salvage only the survivors among those many fresh-coined words and phrases which race for an hour against oblivion. Much of the flash and pertinence of stories told in slang must evaporate as its ephemeral items fall and die. To put the reverse English, as Mr. Ade might pun, on what Ben Jonson said of Shakspere, the fables are not for all time but of an age. Yet they have a promising vitality. After nearly a quarter of a century the earliest among them are still racy, though most of the newspaper laughter of their day has turned rancid or has perished altogether; and the latest show a decided gain upon the earliest in body and significance. Lacking the wings of poetry or readily intelligible wit which carry books to the ends of the earth, they incomparably fit certain phases of their own place and era which cannot be neglected. The comic spirit, hopeful as love and as recurrent as hunger, has its Hoosier incarnation.

PRUDENCE MILITANT

E. W. Howe

IN the annals of America there is a chapter to
be written on the influence of the cross-roads
tavern and the corner grocery. There the neighborhood wits and wise men have regularly come
together, scanning the national horizon and
bringing topics home for local commentary.
They have measured the most complex events by
simple rules; they have wondered and cursed and
laughed that such fuss should be made over far-
away affairs; they have yarned and gossiped;
they have turned universal wisdom into the dry
vernacular; they have helped popular opinions
to be born. Now and then one of these wits and
wise men is something of a poet or a saint, touching the conversation with a little radiance; but
most of them walk close to the smooth path of
common sense. They know only those things
which they have heard many times. They feel

confident about only those things which have been tried, and tried many times. Even when they venture into longer speculations, they venture cautiously. Religion in their talk becomes ethics, government becomes politics, economics becomes business, love becomes obscenity or matrimony, manners become conventions; all the virtues come down to prudence. The heretic among them either shrinks from the stout front which they present or else elaborates his rebellion into a custom which they endure only if he has been prudent in his own life. Partly with incredulity and partly with contempt they greet reports of idealism unless it is idealism standardized and recognized. Everywhere they are the same. As the tavern disappears before prohibition and the corner grocery before the mail-order catalogue, the wits and wise men find new lounging-places, in clubs, in the smoking-rooms of railway trains, in all the minor caucuses of ordinary life. But the channel of folk-disquisition, though thus widened, has not been greatly shifted.

2

Out of this tradition emerges the figure that has most conspicuously of late brought genius to the task of putting rural wisdom into speech. The newspaper which E. W. Howe long owned and edited in Atchison gave him a provincial reputation and made him an independent fortune, but it is for his fiction and for *E. W. Howe's Monthly,* founded after he retired from daily journalism, that he is really known. The steady animus with which he keeps thrusting at men of letters for their folly and uselessness can not disguise the fact that he himself is one of them. Only a man with a powerful urge could have been faithful for a dozen years to the task of writing the whole of a monthly mazagine; only a man with a notable literary gift could have given expression to so much matter in a manner so precise, so lucid, so arresting, so personal. For sheer skill in making words serve him he has no superior and few equals among his contemporaries. He is a master of the difficult trick of the aphorist. And back of this deftness there lies, unquestionably, a store of art and passion. He who is a scourge of wits and poets is himself a wit and a poet. He owes his habit of scourging such fellows to differences in doctrine rather than to differences in temper. He blames them because they rebel too often, he thinks, against the plain and natural order of life.

Yet he has been a rebel in his time. *The Story of a Country Town,* written before Mr. Howe was thirty, was to the novels of its decade what *Moby Dick* had been to the romances of an earlier decade. It broke a pattern and shouldered its way among the fragments. In a year in which Mark Twain with *Life on the Mississippi* and Joel Chandler Harris with *Nights with Uncle Remus* and James Whitcomb Riley with *The Old Swimmin' Hole* were proclaiming the heroic or the quaint or the sentimental qualities of their particular regions, Mr. Howe exhibited his community as cramped and moldy. The men of Twin Mounds were futile, argumentative, boastful, discontented, envious, and mean. They loafed and waited for miracles to happen to them. They invented and spread scandals, they laid claim to wickedness they did not dare to practise, they walked in a stodgy round of orthodoxies. When Mr. Howe wanted to create a personage among them he created Lytle Biggs, who lived to vex the town by saying bitter things about it and about mankind in general. When he wanted to construct a dramatic story he did not know how to find all he needed in the actual life of the neighborhood, but lugged in items which he had picked up from romantic melodrama—a dark wood, a mysteriously tolling bell, chests of curious treasures, hidden identities, murder at a ford. He wrote his novel not, as novels were then being written, in the manner of a more or less comic idyl, but in that of a saga.

His special distinction as a novelist, indeed, is that he has something of that incomparable, irrecoverable art which went into the making of the Icelandic sagas. The likeness seems to lie less in his technic than in his tone. He is curt, downright, conversant with affairs, incapable of superstition, level in speech about the most stirring matters. These traits persisted even when, in *The Anthology of Another Town,* published within a few months of *Main Street,* he returned after nearly forty years to his first theme with a rather greater inclination to miscellaneous gossip. Talking, for instance, about Jim and Dan Ayres, he tells how these two, when boys in Virginia, played truant from Sunday school and went through the woods toward a commotion which they heard beyond, though they were both afraid their father would whip them for running away. "They walked, and walked, and walked. All the time the commotion over beyond the Big Woods became more pronounced, but they couldn't tell what it was. They forded streams, and were chased by strange dogs, but kept on; from ten o'clock in the morning until three o'clock in the afternoon. They had nothing to eat, and they didn't know that they could ever find their way back, because they were in a country strange to them. But they kept on, and a little after three o'clock, as a reward for their perseverance, they walked into the battle of Bull Run." Here the story ends without a word of comment; but in less than two pages of quiet prose it has set a stage and brought to a thrilling climax an action which is alive with historical irony.

In the *Anthology* Mr. Howe still has his old sense of the dullness of most human lives. Once, he says, he went to talk to an old man expecting to hear something memorable and found the old man could recall nothing more worth recalling out of his seventy-seven years than the fact that long ago he had killed a squirrel with a rifle when several men had shot at it and missed. "In his day there were bears and deer and buffaloes, but he never killed one. He was once young and rode about looking for adventures, but never found any. In the early days there were bold and wicked men, but they never disturbed him. For seventy-odd years he has locked his doors and fastened his windows at night, but has never been robbed. In seventy-seven years he has never had an illness worth recalling. The wind and lightning have threatened more than three quarters of a century without hitting him." But if the earlier sense of irony persists, the earlier bitterness is gone. The mayor of the town, after all his efforts to make George Coulter's funeral a success, has to ask who the dead man was; yet the account of the ceremonies, sly with comedy as it is, is also full of a neighborly tolerance for little folk-ways. Mr. Howe, the book makes it seem, has become generously reconciled to the village.

3

This evolution is one of the most interesting things about him, and it calls for some analysis. In the *Story* there are, it is true, certain of the seeds of the *Anthology:* a partiality for simple people, a distrust of all windy philanthropy, a passion for prudence. But another factor must be taken into account. *The Story of a Country Town* made no important noise in the world, and the novels which shortly followed it made still less. A fate which might have awakened in a different man a fresh obstinacy or a feeling of grievance against contemporary taste, had upon Mr. Howe much the effect which was produced upon Benjamin Franklin when that tentative poet was assured by his father that verse-makers were usually beggars. Perhaps, each of these beginners suspected, the world might be right. Franklin, with less passion for anything beside the main chance, found it easier than Mr. Howe to forgive himself for his false start. Mr. Howe, not only more passionate but also more deeply committed, has never quite got over, consciously or unconsciously, blaming himself for those eager days when his imagination moved through spacious, rebellious regions of romance and tragedy. Yet with whatever effort, about which he wrote no lyric and no elegy, he folded his wings, took in sail, gave himself to his newspaper, and set out to understand the world in which he had not succeeded with his fictions. He ended by accepting it, he claims, virtually without reservation.

That is to say, he accepts it for what it is when the common prudence of the human race is allowed to take its natural course. The average man, he likes to argue, is reasonably healthy, sane, kind, discreet, industrious, good, happy, and successful. Such a man, allowed to follow his natural bent in ordinary society, will get something solid out of life and will give something solid to it. The trouble is that he is too seldom let alone. Theology worries him, philosophy fuddles him, poetry beguiles him, government imposes upon him, reform nags him, gossip lies about him. He sees himself lumped with thousands and millions of other men and then labeled with terms which have no real application to him, but which, because they are widely accepted, have an unavoidable bearing upon his career. Though his own problems remain actually simple, he can not see them clearly for the fog of words which has been raised. Though the problems of nations are merely the problems of aggregations of men like himself, and therefore simple, he can not understand them, because he is bewildered by being assured that his public interests are by some mystery different from his private interests. Consequently he finds himself enlisted in wars and movements and crusades, or consecrated to topheavy idealisms, or set adrift in this or that kind of current folly. Mr. Howe defends this natural man against the disturbing wiles of poets and saints, philanthropists and politicians.

In particular, he upholds the economic order

which he believes has in the long run proved most useful and beneficent. The title of one of his books is *The Blessing of Business;* that of another is *Success Easier than Failure;* and these furnish the chief texts for his commentary. "The first principle," he says, "is life; the second is maintenance of life. . . . We live because of our work; and without life we should need neither salvation, learning, literature, nor anything else." To talk about capitalism or socialism is to stick large, vague labels upon what Mr. Howe thinks are the facts of human life. Those facts are, in brief, that a man would rather live than die; that he keeps himself alive by work; that he works best when he is working for himself; that the best society is that in which the most men work best. The arts and the idealisms are, much as artists and idealists like to think otherwise, and delightful as such items of human existence are, luxuries rather than necessities. Why, then, do so many tongues go on clacking against industry and thrift, as if these essential virtues were minor virtues? Look, Mr. Howe insists, at the way they are actually regarded. "In theory, it is not respectable to be rich. In fact, poverty is a disgrace." He does not object to this condition of affairs. Persons who are not sick or old, he has observed, almost invariably owe their property to their unwillingness to work or to save. If there are too many of them in a community, the community suffers. It is better, consequently, for the failures to be punished and for the successes to be rewarded, as they are in the economic order which has been arrived at after thousands of years, than for the failures to be coddled and the successes made to pay the bill. If this looks cruel, it looks so only to the short-sighted. The far-sighted understand that it is merely kindness to the many who do deserve it instead of kindness to the few who on the whole deserve it less.

The bluntness of this language gives the meaning an apparent shortness which it does not have in Mr. Howe's mind. He has a passion for reality which makes it seem to him more stirring and more beautiful than any conceivable fancies or sentiments. He loves most in life those things which he feels to be most alive. He judges the center of human existence to lie in the region of human necessities, and when he contends for them he is contending for existence itself as against the clouds, however pretty, which lie further from the center. He has a feeling for life, whatever the reason may say about it. "I have heard the question asked thousands of times: 'Is life worth living?' It doesn't make any difference whether it is or not; we have it, and must make the best of it. And so long as we do not blow our brains out, we have decided life is worth living." To be thus reconciled to life is positively to love it. Nor does Mr. Howe stop with affection; he goes on to vigorous defense of what he values. Nothing is more effective in his method than the way he carries war into the field of his opponents. In an age when prudence is generally discreet, he makes it militant. At a time when most conservatives are stupid or inarticulate, he has the zest and gusto of the most energetic and pungent radical. Sitting in his farm-house in Atchison, with winter excursions to Florida, he pours out the strong flood of his sharp words in his *Monthly* devoted to "indignation and information." He reads many books, scrutinizes affairs far and wide, and has his say.

4

Mr. Howe's position in the main line of American rural wisdom appears most distinctly in his sense that life is not a complex thing. "I have lived a long time," he says, "and my real prob-

lems have always been simple." So, looking at
the news which comes from Russia, for instance,
or from the industrial communities of the United
States, he measures them by Kansas. In Kansas
if the village loafer and the village atheist should
lead a revolution, there would be trouble; if there
is trouble in Russia, it is because, it seems to Mr.
Howe, some such uprising has been tolerated.
In rural Kansas, prosperous and peaceful, the
economic order is so easy to comprehend and the
occasional suffering from poverty is so likely to
be alleviated by neighborly kindness that it is
hard to see why endless war should be kept up
in the mines and factories of West Virginia and
Pennsylvania. If only people everywhere would
work and save as they have a chance to do in
Kansas, they would be as happy as in Kansas
they have a chance to be. Mr. Howe has never
come to understand the helplessness of crowded
masses of men at certain times when they find
themselves caught in a machine which is too large
for them to control and when they see no way
for them to keep alive except by desperate action.
The necessity and the compulsion of revolution
do not exist for this prudent farmer who can not
imagine a family without food and shelter and
who knows that though the seasons are recurrent

they are not revolutionary. Life, to such a man, is as simple as men will let it be.

If this country way of seeing existence as easier than it always is seems now and then a defect in Mr. Howe, it implies a quality in which he excels most living men. He is singularly incapable of being fooled, because he is quite incapable of being taken in by abstractions and big words. He tests everything by the rule of practice. "There are no mysteries. Where does the wind come from? It doesn't matter: we know the habits of wind after it arrives." As little susceptible to the mystical element of religion as Thomas Paine, he has respect for the good which churches do in helping to make life orderly and decent. Thus he falls into no excesses of faith or doubt. Convinced that most of the fuss and feathers of government are a wasteful nuisance and that "the people are always worsted in an election," he still does not quarrel with the police or with the tax assessors. Impatient enough with folly to say that "the long and the short of it is, whoever catches the fool first is entitled to shear him," Mr. Howe knows the uses of pity. He can be as terrible as Swift about the cruelty of the race, as when he, himself aging, says: "How good we all are, in theory,

[47]

to the old; and how in fact we wish them to wander off like old dogs, die without bothering us, and bury themselves." Yet he has also this to say: "When I was so young there were babies in my family, two of them died in a week and left the house childless. My most distinct memory now, so long after, is the goodness of the neighbors. I forgive the race much because of that recollection." Other wise men may be shrewd till they are hard or good till they are soft, but Mr. Howe, taking his stand at the humane center of life, holds that both shrewdness and goodness belong there.

Simple as his point of view is, his range of topics is great. He can compress centuries of history and character in a sentence: "With women, men are the enemy; I suppose they abuse them as a nation abuses a people with whom it is at war, with old stories told in other wars." He abounds in touches of homely experience: "A loafer never works except when there is a fire; then he will carry out more furniture than anybody." He can utter a confession which challenges all who read it. "I've been ashamed of myself many years because of neglect to accomplish certain things. But lately I am feeling better about it: I have concluded that the tasks

I didn't accomplish, I couldn't accomplish."
Strokes like these make it clear why Mr. Howe
is so effective. Not only does he continue a long
American tradition and sum up a wisdom which
millions of plain men over the country would put
into words if they could snare the words; he has
also the art of expression to an eminent degree
and he speaks out of a depth of personal experience which gives an uncanny authority to his
remarks. Many an old man in the tradition has
sat in his established chair of the cross-roads
tavern or the corner grocery and delivered himself of such wisdom as he had in such words as
he could find. But rarely has one lived so profoundly, so broodingly, so questioningly, or
looked so far as Mr. Howe. His wit, though
that is eminent, could not give him his influence
if it came from a flat or angular personality. He
has the depth and the intensity as well as the
edge of genius.

THE SOIL OF THE PURITANS

Robert Frost

THE Puritans dreamed their dream on an island, but they carried it to a continent. That high city they were to build without hands, that tower which was to touch heaven, that commonwealth of all the virtues—these phases of the dream in some way or other took for granted a barrier around England as powerful as the sea. The barrier did not hold. Animosity awoke in neighbor kingdoms and struck at the Puritans for their daring. Contention at home grew so keen that many of those who were stoutest in the new faith broke the barrier outward and went across the Atlantic to establish a New England more congenial to their doctrine. Here also there was no wall to protect the sacred commune. The colonies and states of New England might bind themselves together with a thousand chains of unity and pride and hope, but a continent

yawned behind them. As the generations fell
away from the radiance of the first vision, they
turned to more and more secular undertakings.
They sailed off to the ends of the earth in busy
ships; they drifted off into the Western wilderness. The original stock was constantly dimin-
ished and diluted. The more adventurous spir-
its begot their children upon the women of distant regions. The dissenters from the native
code of the region enriched other communities
with the heat and stir of their dissent. Those
who remained tended to be either the most successful or the least successful, the gentry for
whom Boston set the mode or the gnarled farmers
who tugged at the stones of inland hillsides.

The gentry found its poetical voice first:
the sharp-tongued satirists of the Revolution;
Holmes, the little wit of the Puritan capital;
Longfellow, the sweet-syllabled story-teller and
translator; Lowell, learned and urbane, who
stooped to the vernacular; Emerson, whose glow-
ing verses had to preach. The Yankee subsoil
long resisted the plow. Thoreau, hired man of
genius, read Greek in his hermitage; Whittier,
born to be the ballad-maker of his folk, was half
politician. And when, after the Civil War, rural
New England was rediscovered by poetry and ro-

mance, it was valued largely because it seemed quaint, because it was full of picturesque remnants of a civilization. For half a century too many of those who sang its charms looked at them as if from the cool verandas of summer boarding-houses, touched by an antique fashion and tickled by an angular dialect. They collected episodes and characters as they collected brass knockers and hooked rugs and banister-back chairs and walnut high-boys. As time went on there were so many summer visitors that they forgot the natives. The rock-bound coast echoed to the cries of jolly bathers; up and down the solid hills dashed motor-cars filled with bright boys and girls as pagan as the youth of Greece; hunters in an alien scarlet took stone walls which it had broken backs to build; somber farm-houses blossomed into pleasant villas; oak-raftered barns turned into studios; churches which had once enshrined the aspirations of devout parishes were kept up by the donations of men and women who valued them chiefly for the quality they gave the landscape. No wonder the elder Yankees had no voice. Inarticulate themselves, both by principle and by habit, they invited obscurity. Overwhelmed by the rush of the new world which had poured over them, they took to the safer hills.

But there were flesh and blood beneath their weather-beaten garments, as there was granite beneath the goldenrod and hardhack about which the visitors babbled; and in time the flesh and blood and granite were reached. If it seems strange that Robert Frost, born in California, should have become the voice of those left behind, it actually is natural enough. New England was in his blood, bred there by many generations of ancestors who had been faithful to its soil. Some racial nostalgia helped draw him back; some deep loyalty to his stock intensified his affection. That affection made him thrill to the colors and sounds and perfumes of New England as no poet had done since Thoreau. He felt, indeed, the pathos of deserted farms, the tragedy of dwindling townships, the horrors of loneliness pressing in upon silent lives, the weight of inertia in minds from which an earlier energy has departed; but there was in him a tough sense of fact which would not let him brood. He drew life from the sight of the sturdy processes which still went on. Unable to see these upland parishes as mere museums of singular customs and idioms, he saw them, instead, as the stages on which, as on any human stage however small or large, there are transacted the universal trage-

[53]

dies and comedies of birth, love, work, hope, despair, death. The same sun shines upon New Hampshire as upon Arcadia or Sicily or Provence or Wessex; the same earth rolls under the feet of men. Suppose, Mr. Frost may be imagined as having thought, New England had a poet who, in the Yankee way, was willing to work with the tools he had upon the materials which lay at hand. Suppose, further, he did not forever apologize for his tools or comment upon the quaintness of his materials, but gave his time to fashioning poems which should be shrewd or wise or beautiful in their own right.

2

To compare Robert Frost, as he has often been compared, with Robert Burns, is to call attention at the outset to a difference between the Yankees and the Scots which has had a great effect upon the difference between these two poets. Burns grew up among a peasantry which sang. Not only were there ballads of the traditionary sort in every chimney-corner, but there were also gay tunes in the air ready for the new words of any new versifier. Even a genius like Burns in even his most characteristic lyrics was likely to owe some of his lines and the mold in which he cast them to old songs of love or laughter or defiance; and he was sure in such cases to owe to the fame of the older songs some part of the prosperity of his own. The ears of his hearers were already prepared for him. In rural New England Robert Frost had no similar advantages. Almost the only tunes which had ever been lifted there had been the dry hymns of the churches. Ballad-making had died out; hilarious catches had rarely been trolled in cheerful taverns; youth did not sing its love, but talked when it did not merely hint. New England since the Revolution has had but one great popular orator; since *Yankee Doodle* only one popular patriotic song has come out of New England. The voice of that region is the voice of reason, of the intellect, of prose, canny or noble; it walks, not flies. There was nothing to teach or to encourage Mr. Frost to ride on the wings of established melodies.

He would not have heeded any such teaching and encouragement, perhaps, being so much an individualist in his speech; but that very individualism was in part a Yankee trait. Yet if he could not lean upon accepted habits of song, he could lean upon accepted habits of talk. Behind all that his poems have to say there is to be heard the sound of a shrewd voice speaking. Here, for instance, is a farmer saying that he has never climbed a mountain at the foot of which he lives:

> "I've always meant to go
> And look myself, but you know how it is:
> It doesn't seem so much to climb a mountain
> You've worked around the foot of all your life.
> What would I do? Go in my overalls,
> With a big stick, the same as when the cows
> Haven't come down to the bars at milking time?
> Or with a shotgun for a stray black bear?
> 'Twouldn't seem real to climb for climbing it."

Though the passage is full of significant reference to the unadventurous and utilitarian attitude of the Yankee rustic, it does not raise its voice to point the reference, but hugs the ground of understatement and casual syntax.

Nor does Mr. Frost leave the idiom or rhythm of common speech behind when he rises to the pitch of aphorism. In *The Death of the Hired Man* the wife is telling her husband that the old laborer has come back:

" 'Warren,' she said, 'he has come home to die:
    You needn't be afraid he'll leave you this time.'

  'Home,' he mocked gently.

> 'Yes, what else but home?

SOIL OF THE PURITANS

It all depends on what you mean by home.
Of course he's nothing to us, any more
Than was the hound that came a stranger to us
Out of the woods, worn out upon the trail.'

'Home is the place where, when you have to go there,
They have to take you in.'

                    'I should have called it
Something you somehow haven't to deserve.' "

These definitions of home, as profound as were
ever spoken, fall from the lips which utter them
without one symptom of rhetorical or poetical
self-consciousness. They have the accents of
folk-speech clarified and ennobled, but clarified
and ennobled by no other art than a poet may
learn from folk-speech itself.

Even when Mr. Frost touches his peaks of
elevation he still talks, not sings.

"So was I once myself a swinger of birches.
And so I dream of going back to be.
It's when I'm weary of considerations,
And life is too much like a pathless wood
Where your face burns and tickles with the cobwebs
Broken across it, and one eye is weeping
From a twig's having lashed across it open.
I'd like to get away from earth awhile
And then come back to it and begin over.
May no fate willfully misunderstand me

And half grant what I wish and snatch me away
Not to return. Earth's the right place for love:
I don't know where it's likely to go better.
I'd like to go by climbing a birch tree,
And climb black branches up a snow-white trunk
Toward heaven, till the tree could bear no more,
But dipped its top and set me down again.
That would be good both going and coming back.
One could do worse than be a swinger of birches."

Though at such moments he has become so much
himself that the rhythm is of course personal
more than it is sectional, it still suggests, in its
cadences, the sly, shy Yankee tongue.

3

If Robert Frost talks as becomes a Yankee
poet, so does he think as becomes one. In particular there is his close attention to the objects
he sees in his chosen world. He seems never to
mention anything that he has merely glanced at.
Whether it is a bit of "highway where the slow
wheel pours the sand"; or "windfalls spiked
with stubble and worm-eaten"; or ice-coated
branches that "click upon themselves as the
breeze rises"; or an "instep arch [that] not only
keeps the ache, [but] keeps the pressure of a
ladder round"; or the frost

SOIL OF THE PURITANS

"that doesn't love a wall,
That sends the frozen-ground-swell under it,
And spills the upper boulders in the sun"

—no matter what the thing is that Mr. Frost's eye has seen, he has seen it with his undivided mind and heart. Moreover, he speaks of mowing, for instance, not as a man might who had seen such work done in another's meadow or picture, but as a mower who has done it himself, alert for stones in the grass and tired at the end of the day. He speaks of a cow in apple time or of a colt left out in the weather not as a member of a humane society, but as a farmer who knows the unruly ways of cows and the nervous ways of horses. He speaks of the dislike of Yankees for being told how they shall do their tasks or of the plight of a woman who faces the coming of madness in a life of unrelieved toil, not as a cynic or a spectator or a philanthropist, but as a neighbor of similar persons, well enough aware of their eccentricities, yet still held close to them by the bonds of a neighborly knowledge and affection.

Now, such knowledge and such affection, characteristic as they may be of Robert Frost as an individual, are also characteristic of his Yankee community. In a neighborhood left behind as this is, deserted by its more ambitious members, overrun by outsiders of another culture, the people have been united by a natural increment of passion for their nook of land. They may complain of the hardships they endure, but they would hunger and sicken if they went away. Thus circumscribed, they have grown ardently familiar with the details of their world. Thus disciplined by loneliness and nearness, they have learned to live together. Thoreau himself, the sharpest observer and the sharpest critic of the common life, was eager to be a good neighbor: he was willing to help work the roads that all men used; he would have been prompt to keep up his fences if he had had any. So Mr. Frost, a good neighbor, has drawn from daily Yankee examples a good deal of what he knows about the practice of poetry and the conduct of life.

In either matter he refuses to be vague. If rapture visits him, it must come in the company of something that can be seen or felt. What is it, he asks himself as he is mowing, that his scythe whispers?

"It was no dream of the gift of idle hours,
Or easy gold at the hand of fay or elf:
Anything more than the truth would have seemed too
   weak
To the earnest love that laid the swale in rows,

[60]

SOIL OF THE PURITANS

Not without feeble-pointed spikes of flowers
(Pale orchises), and scared a bright green snake.
The fact is the sweetest dream that labor knows."

And the fact, he might add, is the truest dream
that poetry knows. Ideas, after all, are but dim
lines drawn through unmapped regions from
fact to fact; when all the facts shall have been
found out, there will be no further need for ideas.
Meanwhile poets understand that the love of
reality is the root of most poetry. Diffuse love
too much, and it loses meaning as well as power;
fix it upon specific things, and they become first
important and then representative. Always Mr.
Frost reaches his magic through the door of ac-
tuality. "Sight and insight," he says, are the
whole business of the poet. Let him see clearly
enough, and understanding will be added.

A single short poem will serve to illustrate Mr.
Frost's poetic method. Two generations of prose
have labored to express the loneliness of New
England winters, the pathos of empty houses, the
desolation of old age, the cruelty of the cold. All
this, and more, Mr. Frost, selecting one case only
and omitting generalization or commentary, has
distilled into fewer than thirty lines.

"All out of doors looked darkly in at him

MANY MINDS

Through the thin frost, almost in separate stars,
That gathers on the pane in empty rooms.
What kept his eyes from giving back the gaze
Was the lamp tilted near them in his hand.
What kept him from remembering what it was
That brought him to that creaking room was age.
He stood with barrels round him—at a loss.
And having scared the cellar under him
In clomping there, he scared it once again
In clomping off;—and scared the outer night,
Which has its sounds, familiar, like the roar
Of trees and crack of branches, common things,
But nothing so like beating on a box.
A light he was to no one but himself
Where now he sat, concerned with he knew what,
A quiet light, and then not even that.
He consigned to the moon, such as she was,
So late-arising, to the broken moon
As better than the sun in any case
For such a charge, his snow upon the roof,
His icicles along the wall to keep;
And slept. The log that shifted with a jolt
Once in the stove, disturbed him and he shifted,
And eased his heavy breathing, but still slept.
One aged man—one man—can't fill a house,
A farm, a countryside, or if he can,
It's thus he does it of a winter night."

The bare details are sufficient. They draw no
sword, they wave no banner; but they steal upon
the reader of the poem as if he were the observer

of the scene, and stir him to insight into the essential drama of the situation by making his sight of it so vivid.

As sight and insight are connected in Mr. Frost's procedure, so are the practice of poetry and the conduct of life. He is neighbor, in a Yankee fashion, both to the things he sees and to the beings he sees into. He can smile, as he does in *Mending Wall,* at the peasant-witted farmer who keeps on repeating that "good fences make good neighbors," even though the maxim is something he has inherited, not discovered, and though at the moment the wall he is working at is useless; yet Mr. Frost only smiles, neither condescending nor philosophizing. He approaches his fellows through the fellowship of labor. In *The Tuft of Flowers* he tells how, once turning the hay in a meadow which another man had mowed before him, he thought with pain that men always are alone, "whether they work together or apart." But coming shortly upon a tuft of flowers which the mower had spared out of his delight in their beauty, the poet could

"feel a spirit kindred to my own;
So that henceforth I worked no more alone.

But glad with him, I worked as with his aid,

And weary, sought at noon with him the shade;

And dreaming, as it were, held brotherly speech
With one whose thought I had not hoped to reach.

'Men work together,' I told him from the heart,
'Whether they work together or apart.' "

In this lyrical apologue Mr. Frost is more explicit than almost anywhere else in his work. As a Yankee he may have too little general humanitarianism to be a patriot of the planet, but he is so much a neighbor that he can strike hands of friendship with the persons whom he encounters in his customary work. Other men may make wider acquaintances; other men may have, or feign, wider sympathies; for himself, he will continue to study what lies nearest him, confident that though remoter things may be larger, nearer things are surer.

4

Once Robert Frost's Yankee rhythm and Yankee attitude have been detected, his other qualities become less elusive. Has he failed to represent the whole of humanity in his work? He has not undertaken to do that. He has written about the things that interest him most. Has he found much of life drab and lonely? He has merely set down what he saw. At least, he has not been morbid. He is full of quiet fun, of the sense of windy pastures, of spicy roadside smells, of hardy souls busily at work, of drama unfolding naturally out of the movements of life. He dives into the Yankee back country and brings up fierce tales of sin and witchcraft; he dives into the Yankee character and brings up a cranky humor as well as a stern gravity, a longing for freedom and beauty and love as well as a deliberate endurance of hard fate. Puritan as his tradition may be, he singularly lacks the Puritan modes of judgment, and he sets forth departures from the common codes of Yankee life without rancor. He manages to seem to be a poet talking about his neighbors and still to be minding his own business. He is, to risk a paradox, both closer to his folk than are the summer visitors and further from it. That is, he is so close as not to think of explaining Yankees to the world, and so far as not to be sentimental about them.

Or, to put the matter in more literary terms, Robert Frost has given little of his power to commentary and much of it to creation. For this reason he suffers with that larger audience which a poet can hardly catch without doing something

to digest his own work for it.   In the long run,
however, he has taken the better road.   The New
England temper has ordinarily thought that in
literature it is better to comment than to create;
it has produced more sermons than poems.   Even
Thoreau, whom Mr. Frost most resembles among
New-Englanders, though he lived a life as clear-
cut as that of some hero in a book, did not create
such a person.   He talked about his time without
bodying it forth; he believed that he could tell
the world more about Concord by discussing it
and the world at large than by portraying some
typical Yankee character or mood or drama.
Mr. Frost has gone back of this discursive habit
to the true way of the old Yankees themselves,
as if he were the last of the Yankees and their
essence; he has as a poet taken a leaf out of the
book of men and women who would rather talk
than sing, but who would also rather work than
talk.

THE GREAT AND GOOD
TRADITION

Stuart P. Sherman

FOR whatever reasons, the universities in the United States no longer put such a shoulder to the wheel of creative literature as they put there half a century or so ago. No poet of the relative eminence of Longfellow, no wit of the relative eminence of Holmes, no critic of the relative eminence of Lowell, is now also a professor. The gulf which, in retrospect, appears to have divided these reputable citizens from Emerson and Hawthorne and Thoreau, as well as from Poe and Whitman, has grown wider and has caused new alinements, until creative writers and scholars alike seem often to forget that beyond the gulf from each of them there is another side concerned with letters. The scholars spend their talents, often admirable, on antiquarian research, but rarely know or care enough to encourage, interpret, or preserve the best that is being done from year to year. The creative writers know or care little about antiquarian research and not much more about those kinds of learning which alone can impart certain of the most solid merits to masterpieces. In creative circles it is regarded as singular that Robert Frost intermittently and Robert Herrick persistently hold professorships; in professorial circles it is commonly thought best, when an active poet or novelist is added to the staff of a university, to keep him below the salt with the instructors or among the side shows with the extension lecturers. Doubtless there is no cure for this division. Chaucer, Shakespeare, Milton, Fielding, Wordsworth, Dickens, Hardy, were not professors; nor, for that matter, have many of the great critics been: Dryden, Johnson, Hazlitt, Carlyle, Emerson, as against Arnold and Saintsbury, who both wore their academic mantles lightly. Doubtless the men of imagination will go on hacking at their own sweet wills, and the men of erudition will go on carefully gathering up the chips when they are dry. It seems a pity.

2

In the United States, however, there is one professor who does not fit comfortably into this scheme. The experimenters who have felt the lash of Stuart P. Sherman, as most experimenters have at one time or another, might possibly like it better if they could accuse him of the common academic sins of dullness or of ignorance of what is current. Unfortunately, he commits neither of these sins. He is both a poet and a wit, with a robust and dramatic energy, and he can write as few of his contemporaries can. If he has slain Theodore Dreiser with a violent right hand, he has with a gentler left given the accolade to Sinclair Lewis. Of those who honor Whitman, he lifts one of the most impassioned voices. Even H. L. Mencken, his principal antagonist, pays Mr. Sherman frequent tributes for his style and for his power. Yet though he does not actually fit into the established scheme, he has been made to fit into it by an increasing legend which, fixed by his *On Contemporary Literature,* assigns him to the general's command over the forces of reaction. This he owes in a considerable measure to his trick of nagging the new generation in almost every paragraph. As young himself as many of those whom he accuses of being young, he affects the staff and slipper, though he has plenty of muscle with which to smite and spank. Perhaps it is because of his own youth that he is so impatient with those who share and mirror it. An anonymous critic has pointed out that Mr. Sherman, already famous and a full professor at thirty, had no chance to take advantage of his twenties. "From the first," says that critic, "responsibility has sat upon his shoulders. He has been a pillar, an arbiter, a last resort, a throne. He has had to walk cautiously among the elder statesmen of his bailiwick; he has had to assume maturity to match his power over his numerous subordinates. Compelled to administer and to account for his administration, he has been too busy ever to have the fling which his years deserved." No wonder, concludes his critic, that Mr. Sherman has learned to act "as if each new author were some raw sophomore badly in need of a perspiring session on the diaconal carpet."

The matter goes deeper than mere discipline. For teachers there is always the temptation to become contentious partizans of older modes of thinking and feeling. Something of this temptation shows in Mr. Sherman's critical technic. For instance, now that Puritanism is under fire from various quarters, he can write thus in his latest book: "Puritanism, rightly understood, is one of the vital, progressive, and enriching human traditions. It is a tradition peculiarly nec-

essary to the health and the stability and the safe
forward movement of a democratic society." Yet
half a dozen years ago, before the attack upon
Puritanism had reached the surface of ordinary
discussion and when that strenuous spirit was indeed regularly praised by the common lip, Mr.
Sherman in his *Matthew Arnold* held a different
position: "In countries like England and the
United States, where an ideal of spiritual perfection, and an inadequate ideal of spiritual perfection, has been established by the English
Puritans, nothing could be more timely, more
salutary, then Arnold's respectful yet vigorous
exposure of that ideal." This contradiction in a
commentator not generally thought of as fickle
will mystify no man or woman who has looked
from the professional rostrum out over challenging young faces and has felt the need of combat-
ing their newest prejudices by proving that there
is something still to be said for prejudices not
so new. Mr. Sherman has felt the need and has
yielded to it, at first partly out of disposition to
argue and later out of a disposition to defend
himself when his volleys were returned.

But even deeper than his nagging language
and his pedagogic method lies an experience
which points the way at last to the central stuff

of Mr. Sherman's constitution. That same anonymous critic of his has put a trustworthy, if flippant, finger upon the experience: "Let no one think that Sherman has always been a pillar of his state. In his Harvard days, grubbing among the grammars into which the system forced him, he swore dreadfully. There he discovered the austerity of Pater and the softness of Thoreau: there he ransacked the decadents, from purple Rome to yellow Nineties, and specialized in the more immoral Elizabethans; once done with Harvard, he bludgeoned its manner of literary study till the welkin shook. The philologers then hated him like vulgar poison. The recalcitrant among the scholars then rallied round him. So, too, when he first went to Illinois from Massachusetts, he was full of brash irreverences, an æsthete stranded in a village, homesick Ovid among the honest Goths. Where another man would have flown the coop in irritation, Sherman buried himself in Boswell's *Johnson* and learned how to rule a clucking roost. He buried himself in Burke and learned how, while distrusting revolutions, to fit his stride to the progress of a race. He buried himself in Matthew Arnold and learned how to test all things by the best." Yes, and he buried himself in Sherman, and found

there a weariness after controversy, a longing for
security among the wrangles of the senses and
the debates of the passions, a desire to live safely
in some great and good tradition.

3

The war drew him out of his private literary
studies to the consideration of American ideals
and of the place of national societies in human
life. Into all that Mr. Sherman wrote under
the shadow of the noise of battles it is no longer
quite fair to go; he caught the prevailing fever
and he occasionally, like many smaller men,
raved. But it is necessary to say something
about the process by which he who had always
been such a foe to chauvinism came to the point
where his writings might be cited, though not always justly, to give aid and comfort to chauvinists. Outraged by certain stupid and arrogant
types of German propaganda, which claimed for
the German element in American culture a gro-
tesquely larger share than it has contributed, he
set out to discover, for purpose of counter-
propaganda, the tap-root of the national genius,
the true history of the national soul. As a man
of letters he followed into the past the trail of the
written word, finding, of course, that the widest,

most beaten, and least interrupted trail led to
Plymouth Rock. As an inheritor of the line of
men and women who had used the trail, he found
himself warmed and lifted by the fiery words of
the fathers, by the noble and humane words of
all the intermediate sons. Convinced that here
were the tap-root and history he was looking for,
Mr. Sherman deduced from them those large
views of American polity and destiny for which
he is in this decade the most eloquent spokesman.
"If even for a moment," he has subsequently explained, "it occurred to me that true citizenship
in 'the country of all intelligent beings' might
necessitate the sacrifice of one's essential Americanism and the use of the knife at the root of all
fond sentiments related to it, in that instant there
came to me, as if in a vision, our 'divine mother,'
the spirit of America as the clear-eyed among our
poets and statesmen have seen her, assuring me
that the higher piety demands no such immola-
tion. That which we have loved in our country,
she declared, that which we have honored in her,
that which reveals her to our hearts as profoundly
beautiful is in no way dangerous to humanity.
On the contrary, the more deeply we loved the
true constituent elements of her loveliness, the
more clearly we understood her inmost purposes

and set ourselves to further them, the more perfectly we should find ourselves in accord with
the 'friends of mankind' in all nations."

That is to say, Mr. Sherman had found a cause
in which he believed that the poet, the philosopher, and the politician in him could join hands
without strife. This sense of his cause increased
the Olympian in his attitude. He who had de-
fended the classics against all challengers by reminding the challengers that they were little
better than sophomores after all, now answered
the critics of America by reminding them that
they were only Jews or Germans, clowns or in-
ternationalists, and as such were incapable of understanding, as the purer strains could do, the
great meaning, the great goal, of the republic.
This shift of Mr. Sherman's played happily into
the hands of the chauvinists, who found it easy
to overlook what their new ally had to say, for
instance, about the uglier aspects of Roosevelt,
and easier still to catch from *Americans* and *The
Genius of America* the general implication that
the course of the nation has had at once a Roman
grandeur and a Puritan rectitude. No wonder
the chauvinists promptly clutched and steadily
continue to clutch at these consoling doctrines.
Around them has been growing up a generation

which denies that the progress of the United
States can be interpreted in the terms of a Vir-
gilian epic; which insists upon the contrast between the public utterances and the actual behavior of the statesmen in charge of American
foreign policy, between the gestures of domestic
comity and the actual treatment of racial and
political minorities, between the accepted notions
of native efficiency and the actual facts of
looseness and corruption in public affairs. Mr.
Sherman ought to know that the life of any nation must be seen now and then as an ironic
comedy. He does know it, for he is a man of
shrewd and realistic perceptions; but for the moment he is riding the high horse of the grand
style and rocking to sleep that comic spirit, which
also feels the "fond sentiments" related to patriotism and yet insists upon distinctions among
them. Meanwhile the national Pharisees rejoice.

4

They have probably less reason for rejoicing
than they think they have. Mr. Sherman is not
one of those critics who sullenly stand still, nurs-
ing their first, and last, convictions. But a few
years ago he was inclined to distrust democracy

with his favorite teacher, Paul Elmer More; now
he upholds that mode of government at all hours.
But a few years ago he feared the expansive passions with his other teacher, Irving Babbitt; now
he thrills with the average man at the sight of his
country's flag. But a few years ago he agreed
with Matthew Arnold that Shakespeare and Virgil
would have been bored, as Mr. Sherman would
then have been, in the company of the Pilgrim
Fathers; now he elects those saints and their con-
geners to the great society of good men who in all
ages have sought perfection and thus saved the
world alive. It is on this last point that he has
been most explicit. Once his Puritans were conservatives, planted on the hard soil of a stubborn
code while the rest of mankind were moving away
toward the green valleys of reasonableness and
sweetness; now they are radicals, tearing themselves away from the mean and customary without thought of the consequences to the human
organism which they disrupt. Mr. Sherman,
sore at the accusations of Puritanism leveled
against him, has even carried the war into the
territory of his enemies by arguing that his enemies are less radical than his Puritans, mere
striplings bent upon the introduction of a new

and superficial fashion which will allow them all to conform to it and yet not worry about their deeper consciences.

This is dangerous territory. A critic must be singularly incapable of growth if he is to remain satisfied forever with the praise of dead radicals. In time Mr. Sherman may find himself as much shocked as some of his admirers are at his list of the companions to whom he turns when he is asked to help his generation escape from the evils it finds unendurable: "Those of the great society, as wise men from Cicero to Ruskin have reminded us, have poets, emperors, priests, philosophers, saints, and sages for their table companions and for the familiars of their peopled solitude—all who for one great reason or another have merited eternal life. The ideal world in which these presences move seems to our warm youth, eager for sensuous contacts, somewhat cold and insubstantial; but as we advance in age and discover the fickle and transitory character and the emptiness of many of our relationships with those who seem to be living, and, on the other hand, the fidelity and permanence and richness of our relationships with those who seemed to be dead, then the ideal world begins to grow upon us, and its presences appear to our clearer

perception to be the objects in our consciousness
of the most indisputable reality. Then indeed
we know that Socrates and Cicero are with us;
St. Paul and Augustine and Aquinas; Petrarch
and Machiavelli; Shakespeare, Bacon, Milton,
and Bunyan; Descartes and Locke; Voltaire and
Rousseau and Burke and Goethe; Franklin and
Adams and Lincoln, Emerson, Whitman, and
Mark Twain." In the name of the gods of justice and of all the sons of reason everywhere, Mr.
Sherman's admirers may well ask, by what right
does a moralist who instinctively resists all in-
novation venture to sit down and take his ease
by the side of a Whitman who spent his life
fighting official censorship and academic neglect,
by the side of a Voltaire who ate his bread in
exile from his own land because he could not
agree with its great tradition, by the side of a
Paul who chose and preached a new religion in
the teeth of desperate perils, by the side of a
Socrates whom the conservatives in the most brilliant period of human history put to death because he held opinions with which they had not
yet caught up? It might be reasonable for Mr.
Sherman to include such persons in his society
of loved companions if he viewed all life as a
dramatic spectacle upon which the wise man

should look coolly, savoring its tragedy with its comedy, yet disinclined to expect one outcome more than another; it is unreasonable for Mr. Sherman at once to approve the rebellions of the dead and to disapprove the rebellions of the living.

5

He would answer, of course, that most innovations are not important, and that it is no less the duty of a true critic to expose the trivial than to aid the weighty ones. He would further answer, possibly, that the present age is mad and whirling, strayed as in the night from its standards, lost in a tangle of blind doubt and fruitless experiment. Well, to the conservative instinct all ages look like that. And, to be completely dispassionate, the radical instinct is habitually curt with many things which are precious and which in the end survive the most iconoclastic maulings. Part of the test of the valuable critic, however, is not his general doctrine, but his specific deeds. Mr. Sherman has for fifteen years been an outstanding figure in American criticism. In that time he has had to his public credit the discovery of not one single beginner in the arts, the defense of only one single new reputation—

and it the reputation of Sinclair Lewis, whom
the rest of the world was acclaiming, too. Even
in his treatment of Whitman Mr. Sherman has
curiously insisted on lugging that large spirit
into the Puritan fold, and in his treatment of
Mark Twain has blandly insisted on under-
emphasizing the naturalistic pessimism which
gives much of the essential salt to Mark Twain's
humor. With regard to every novel scheme for
governing mankind or for solving the problems
of the economic life Mr. Sherman has resolutely
held his tongue. The question is simply whether
the age and its convictions and its tendencies are
as barren as he has managed to make out. If
they are, he has wasted his great strength in trying to break wild asses which had better been left
among their congenial thistles.

The discussion, however, forces its way round
again to the contradiction between Mr. Sherman's
passion for striking whatever new head shows
itself and his other passion for arguing that the
quest for perfection is the driving force of life.
That contradiction goes back in him to the difficulty which he has experienced of reconciling his
instinct to cling to what is tried and to shrink
from what is untried, with his reason, which,
helped by historical investigations, assures him

that established ideas and procedures pass and that new ones take their place. If his instinct continues to have its way with him, and grows upon him, it may in the end be able to enlist him in the old guard forever, with the morose regiments of Americanism and fundamentalism. Yet certain of his readers, loyal against many odds, still hold to the belief that Mr. Sherman will some day integrate his instinct with his reason and will become the voice and guide which his capacities could make him; that he will promote youth to the side of age in the company of things worth reverence.

THE TOWER OF IRONY

George Santayana

WHILE there was still a school of philosophy
at Harvard, it had thinkers and teachers
so diverse in their philosophical attitudes that
they hardly seemed to constitute a school at all;
yet possibly they were, on that account, but the
more representative of the loosely federated phi-
losophies which make up the republic of American
speculative thought. Was there not in the Harvard group that gracious connoisseur of beauty
and goodness, George Herbert Palmer, who with
mellow piety carried on the line of Puritanism
as softened in the neighborhood of Boston by
secular culture? Was there not Josiah Royce,
summoned from California with his new proof
of the existence of God and the vast learning with
which he, thanks in part to his German masters,
built up the ample, if involved, structure of metaphysical idealism so much of which labored to

relate the individual to the world as he is related
to it in Christian theology? Was there not William James, brilliant and vernacular, who found
the broadest grounds for the characteristic optimism of his countrymen and did as much as can
be done to introduce the studious cell and the
strenuous market-place to each other? And was
there not George Santayana, lent to the New
World by Spain, who looked through Catholic
eyes at Puritanism, through Hellenic eyes at
Christianity, through skeptic eyes at democracy
and optimism? In this charming variety were
met elements which have so rarely come together
in any university that the episode of their association must long continue to interest the historian and critic. Particularly must the historian or critic of literature be excited by the presence in the Harvard group of its youngest member and its finest genius.

2

Mr. Santayana was first of all a poet, imagin-
ing as well as thinking his way into the lovely
and subtle universe which he inhabits. He himself has given the best analysis of his poetical
qualities: "Of impassioned tenderness or Dio-

nysiac frenzy I have nothing, nor even of that
magic and pregnancy of phrase—really the creation of a fresh idiom—which marks the high
lights of poetry. Even if my temperament had
been naturally warmer, the fact that the English
language (and I can write no other with assur-
ance) was not my mother-tongue would of itself
preclude any inspired use of it on my part; its
roots do not quite reach to my centre. I never
drank in in childhood the homely cadences and
ditties which in pure spontaneous poetry set the
essential key. I know no words redolent of
the wonder-world, the fairy-tale, or the cradle.
Moreover, I am city-bred, and that companion-
ship with nature, those rural notes, which for
English poets are almost inseparable from poetic
feeling, fail me altogether. Landscape to me is
only a background for fable or a symbol for fate,
as it was to the ancients; and the human scene itself is but a theme for reflection. Nor have I
been tempted into the by-ways even of towns, or
fascinated by the aspect and humours of all sorts
and conditions of men. My approach to language is literary." Nevertheless, Mr. Santayana
continues, "In one sense I think that my verses,
mental and thin as their texture may be, represent a true inspiration, a true docility. A Muse

—not exactly an English Muse—actually visited me in my isolation; the same, or the ghost of the same, that visited Boethius or Alfred de Musset or Leopardi. It was literally impossible for me then not to re-echo her eloquence. When that compulsion ceased, I ceased to write verses. My emotion—for there was genuine emotion—faded into a sense that my lesson was learned and my troth plighted; there was no longer any occasion for this sort of breathlessness and unction. I think the discerning reader will probably prefer the later prose versions of my philosophy; I prefer them myself, as being more broadly based, saner, more humorous. Yet if he is curious in the matter he may find the same thing here nearer to its fountain-head, in its accidental early setting, and with its most authentic personal note."

Only at the moment when Mr. Santayana's philosophy was on the anvil did his poetry ring with a note which was either authentic or personal. His convivial and occasional verses are most of them merely painful, his dramatic undertakings bloodless. Now and then in his odes, however, and frequently in his sonnets there is a rapture which stings and haunts and a music which vibrates in a manner wholly alien to inferior verse. For if he was making a philosophy he was also recording the profounder experiences which colored it. His early experience, the record testifies, was largely disentanglement: he freed himself from the ancient faith he had inherited, from his hunger for a love he had failed to win. Custom, sentiment, distrust of knowledge and reason—these held him and tormented him in the matter of his faith, but eventually he overcame them.

> "Sweet are the days we wander with no hope
> Along life's labyrinthine trodden way,
> With no impatience at the steep's delay,
> Nor sorrow at the swift-descended slope.
> Why this inane curiosity to grope
> In the dim dust for gems' unmeaning ray?
> Why this proud piety, that dares to pray
> For a world wider than the heaven's cope?
> Farewell, my burden! No more will I bear
> The foolish load of my fond faith's despair,
> But trip the idle race with careless feet.
> The crown of olive let another wear;
> It is my crown to mock the runner's heat
> With gentle wonder and with laughter sweet."

In the matter of his love, the poet of these sonnets, torn less by his senses than by his hunger for the glory and beauty of loving and being loved—

MANY MINDS

"But, O ye beauties I must never see,
How great a lover have you lost in me!"—

disentangles himself from his hope, which is un-
availing, and from his pain, which long seems
unending, to find at last a refuge beyond all hope
or pain.

"After grey vigils, sunshine in the heart;
After long fasting on the journey, food;
After sharp thirst, a draught of perfect good
To flood the soul, and heal her ancient smart.
Joy of my sorrow, never can we part;
Thou broodest o'er me in the haunted wood,
And with new music fill'st the solitude
By but so sweetly being what thou art.
He hath who made thee perfect, makes me blest.
O fiery minister, on mighty wings
Bear me, great love, to mine eternal rest.
Heaven it is to be at peace with things;
Come chaos now, and in a whirlwind's rings
Engulf the planets. I have seen the best."

Thus the lover, like the thinker of the sonnets
before him, reached a central certitude, a skeptical stability, on which to found his philosophy.
A philosophy so arrived at has little chance to
be shallow, because it has come through experience felt to the roots of life; it has little chance

to be bitter or malicious or complaining, because it has lost its petty selfishness in the furnace of pain. If Mr. Santayana is one of the most logical of philosophers, he is nevertheless one of the most personal, and the two qualities unite to make him, what few human beings are, at once almost equally alive and reasonable.

3

The *Sonnets,* most exquisite verse published in the United States during the noisy nineties, mark, it may be guessed, the period of Mr. Santayana's career in which he had his vision of the reasonable life and made his resolution to build a structure of philosophy which should be worthy of it. All around him lay, he saw, the ruins of idealisms and illusions, the shards of doctrines, tumbled hither and thither by instincts which philosophers were too seldom able to identify or willing to admit to their systems. Man was an animal who by sometimes taking thought had raised himself to a point at which he seemed something more than an animal; but he had still to carry the old load of his instincts and the accumulation and detritus of the various opinions which at different times had served him or hampered him. His intellectual plight was consequently as con-

[89]

fusing, probably, as it had ever been, and he could disentangle himself only by an effort comparable to that by which primitive man had seceded from the beasts who were his neighbors and cousins. Now, however, man must make use, in such an effort, of history as well as of the fumbling analysis and the accidental discovery which had once been his only tools. What Mr. Santayana set out to do was to write, with metaphysical precision, the epic of the mind in its progression from those dim moments when it first became conscious of itself as an entity not hopelessly involved in the mechanism of external nature and of animal instincts, to those other moments, as yet reached by only a handful of the wisest men, when the mind might see itself to be pure intelligence and nature to be pure mechanism. The epic would be a kind of tragi-comedy of errors, struggling against long odds and innumerable defeats to an ending which would be measurably happy.

That *The Life of Reason* took no such form or method as Shelley's *Prometheus Unbound* or *Hellas,* which had sprung from a vision less unlike Mr. Santayana's than may at first glance appear, was due to both Mr. Santayana's temperament and his profession. Temperamentally he was not a "finished child of nature," as he says Shelley was, but "a joint product . . . of nature, history, and society," neither "obtuse to the droll, miscellaneous lessons of fortune," nor incapable of being instructed by the "cannonade of hard, inexplicable facts that knocks into most of us what little wisdom we have." He had to take into account, in his epic, countless items of existence which Shelley was obliged to brush aside if he was to be true to his conception of human life as a dramatic conflict between deliberate evil and deliberate good. Professionally, Mr. Santayana was a philosopher, whose science was dialectic. However vividly he had seen his vision of the rise of the intellect from its first estate, he could no more do justice to it by any merely poetical utterance than a botanist could do justice to a field of flowers by describing his sentiments at the sight of it without mentioning a single flower by name or distinguishing accurately among the odors and colors which to the amateur might seem one delightful picture and no more. Philosopher and botanist both have experts to convince no less than laymen to persuade; they must be analytical and precise. Mr. Santayana, therefore, though he was writing what was in effect an epic, had to make it as exact as a treatise, with the result, natural enough, that the experts have found it too poetic for their taste and the laymen too scientific. *The Life of Reason* has lamentably suffered the fate of Thomas Hardy's *Dynasts,* the sole achievement of any such scope in their English or American generation, and has fallen, as the vulgar say, between two stools.

Its fate is lamentable, for *The Life of Reason* offers a profound, shrewd, stirring, and beautiful synthesis of human existence. Its perspective, if not the longest, is very long. Aided among modern philosophers chiefly by Spinoza, Mr. Santayana goes back to Plato and Aristotle and, disregarding as far as possible all the confusions let into philosophy since their time, establishes his system on grounds which might, he feels, have seemed rational to them. He demolishes and dismisses, as unimportant to the moral philosopher in any case, the speculative doubt as to the existence of reality itself behind appearance. He agrees with Aristotle that "everything ideal has a natural basis and everything natural an ideal development." Thus liberated from fatal prejudices in favor of either nature or the ideal, he proceeds with his history, which is his system in operation, of human nature in pursuit of its ideal desires, by and during the pursuit turning the headlong instinct for reproduction into radiant love, turning blind or superstitious industry into creative art, turning brute gregariousness into that exalted society, transcending clans or states or even utopias, in which "ideal interests take possession of the mind" and "its companions are the symbols it breeds for excellence, beauty, and truth." He studies at length, finally, the three principal elements of ideal society: religion, art, and science. "Religion is the life of the moral imagination, in which poetry and spirituality, God and immortality are the metaphors of man's ideal good. Art is the artifice by which men realize in matter, through sound and sight, in music and in monuments, transitive embodiments of conceived perfection. Science is the transcript in which they foreshorten for practice and convenience an experience which would otherwise be too fluid and anarchic to be dealt with at all."

"I was," Mr. Santayana has since explained, "utterly without the learning and the romantic imagination that might have enabled some emancipated rival of Hegel, some systematic Nietzsche or some dialectical Walt Whitman to write a history of the Will to Be Everything, and Anything. An omnivorous spirit was no spirit for me, and I could not write the life of reason without distinguishing it from madness." The lines he drew between reason and madness reveal the kind of man he was when he was writing his great work. Exiled among protestant, eclectic barbarians, he remembered the sacred Mediterranean, with its memories of Greek freedom and Roman pride and Catholic patience, with its perfect sadness and perennial beauty. Thus remembering, he was sustained by a tradition which had so long seen nature in the background of life that it had come to think it further back than it possibly is. Thus sustained, he could have a more positive conception of the life of reason than he has now, when he has come to think of it as "a decidedly episodical thing, polyglot, interrupted, insecure" and to wonder whether he might not as well have called his book *The Romance of Wisdom*. It is a consequence and a disadvantage of his earlier positiveness that he could once have laid hands so boldly upon anthropology and history and have treated them occasionally as plastic materials to be shaped by creative hands. But so is it a consequence, and an advantage, that he could, without waiting too late to be willing to begin, once have carried his structure to logical completeness and have left a monument of wisdom and beauty which does not suffer too seriously because there are flaws in its details or even because its total plan might have been different. To build he had to choose; no philosopher, as no architect, is universal. A temple may be superb though there is a church next door to it and a railroad station across the way.

Let the synthesis of *The Life of Reason,* however, be challenged as it may, there must remain unchallenged the pertinence and grace and wit of a thousand observations upon human nature which it incidentally makes. "Fanaticism," for instance, "consists in redoubling your effort when you have forgotten your aim." "The intelligent man known to history flourishes within a dullard and holds a lunatic in leash. . . . Thus the best human intelligence is still decidedly barbarous; it fights in heavy armour and keeps a fool at court." Or again: "Pain is consciousness at once intense and empty, fixing attention on what contains no character, and arrests all satisfactions without offering anything in exchange. The horror of pain lies in its intolerable intensity and its intolerable tedium. It can accordingly be cured either by sleep or by entertainment.

[95]

In itself it has no resource; its violence is quite helpless and its vacancy offers no expedients by which it might be unknotted and relieved." At times Mr. Santayana can rise to a wisdom as high and musical as this: "The universe, so far as we can observe it, is a wonderful and immense engine; its extent, its order, its beauty, its cruelty, makes it alike impressive. If we dramatise its life and conceive its spirit, we are filled with wonder, terror, and amusement, so magnificent is that spirit, so prolific, inexorable, grammatical, and dull. Like all animals and plants, the cosmos has its own way of doing things, not wholly rational nor ideally best, but patient, fatal, and fruitful. Great is this organism of mud and fire, terrible this vast, painful, glorious experiment. Why should we not look on the universe with piety? Is it not our substance? Are we made of other clay? All our possibilities lie from eternity hidden in its bosom. It is the dispenser of all our joys. We may address it without superstitious terrors; it is not wicked. It follows its own habits abstractedly; it can be trusted to be true to its word. Society is not impossible between it and us, and since it is the source of all our energies, the home of all our happiness, shall we not cling to it and praise it, seeing that it vegetates so grandly and sadly, and that it is not for us to blame it for what, doubtless, it never knew that it did? Where there is such infinite and laborious potency there is room for every hope. If we should abstain from judging a father's errors or a mother's foibles, why should we pronounce sentence on the ignorant crimes of the universe, which have passed into our own blood?" At times he can, purring, put out a feline claw worthy of Anatole France: "When on the day of judgment, or earlier, a man perceives that what he thought he was doing for the Lord's sake he was really doing for the least, perhaps, of the Lord's creatures, his satisfaction, after a moment's surprise, will certainly be very genuine."

4

Mr. Santayana's other books may be called, not too loosely, commentaries upon *The Life of Reason* or extensions of the theme into areas a little outside its principal terrain. His earlier prose works, *The Sense of Beauty* and *Interpretations of Poetry and Religion,* studied the ways of the spirit in the world of taste and imagination. In *Three Philosophical Poets* and in a famous essay in *Winds of Doctrine* he examined the versions of life which appear in Lucretius, Dante, Goethe, and Shelley, with reference particularly to the relations of civilized philosophy and great poetry. In *Winds of Doctrine,* where he dissected such contemporary thinkers as Bergson and Bertrand Russell, Mr. Santayana first gave his account, now classic, of the two strains, one genteel and pallid, one barbarous and lusty, which make up American philosophy. By this time he had left the United States for Europe, drawn thither by a nostalgia much like that which had earlier drawn Henry James. England had captivated another pilgrim because it seemed to him, and seems, like the inaccessible ancient country in which he would like to have been born. "What I love in Greece and in England is contentment in finitude, fair outward ways, manly perfection and simplicity." Without any inclination to change his nationality, regarding that, no less than religion and love, as a thing "too radically intertwined with our moral essence to be changed honourably, and too accidental to the free mind to be worth changing," he found that in England he could live most comfortably in the broad stream of the life of reason. At the outbreak of the war he joined a more general chorus than he had ever joined before and

baited the Germans with his witty, malicious
Egotism in German Philosophy, a philosophy
which of course he had always looked upon as
barbarian both for its transcendentalism and for
its technical jargon. Subsequently, in *Character and Opinion in the United States,* he looked
back, from the meridian of England, upon the
intellectual and moral life of a nation which had,
he said, "a fund of vigour, goodness, and hope
such as no nation ever possessed before," but
which still, being strenuous and obstreperous,
lacked much of what is best and beautiful.

Mr. Santayana can be sentimental, as in certain passages of his *Soliloquies in England and
Later Soliloquies* wherein he now and then grows
as tender as Washington Irving over the beauties of that happy island. As a writer, he must
be said, for all his pungency, to lack emphasis.
He moves through his discourse with a level, almost a stealthy, gait, without the dramatic moments which philosophy may have no less than
poetry or history. To his fellows of the philosophic guild he seems now too oracular, now too
concrete. But whether sentimental, unemphatic,
or difficult for philosophers, he is essentially all
of one piece. "I notice," he says with some
pride, "that men of the world, when they dip into

my pages, find them consistent, almost oppressively consistent." And rightly, for, as he elsewhere says, "I am resigned to being a mind." By this resignation he has disentangled himself, as far as any philosopher of his time, from instincts, passions, prejudices, doctrines, creeds. Can a man be completely civilized in the midst of a world which is largely animal and barbarous? Mr. Santayana has tried to be that. It is significant that his effort has taken him nearly round a full circle. In his recent *Scepticism and Animal Faith,* wherein he bases a solid confidence in "animal faith" (common sense) upon the complete skepticism which finds only the world of essence indubitable and so regards the world of existence as doubtless illusory but none the less habitable to any who will accept, study, and use the rules by which it is seen to work, he says this in the preface to what he has called his new system of philosophy: "My system is not mine, nor new. . . . I have a great respect for orthodoxy; not for those orthodoxies which prevail in particular schools or nations, and which vary from age to age, but for a certain shrewd orthodoxy which the sentiment and practice of laymen maintain everywhere. I think that common sense, in a rough dogged way, is technically sounder than the special schools of philosophy, each of which squints and overlooks half the facts and half the difficulties in its eagerness to find in some detail the key to the whole. I am animated by distrust of all high guesses, and by sympathy with the old prejudices and workaday opinions of mankind; they are ill expressed, but they are well grounded." On such a platform Aristotle and any plain man can shake hands. Possibly there has been a good deal of error in the notion that Mr. Santayana is a kind of Don Quixote of philosophy, riding on a speculative trail and mistaking solid windmills for dangerous giants. Possibly he will turn out to have been, with his canny wisdom, something of a philosophical Sancho Panza, too.

II. NEW GROWTHS

YOUTH AND WINGS

Edna St. Vincent Millay

THE little renaissance of poetry which there
have been a hundred historians to scent
and chronicle in the United States during the
last decade flushed to a dawn in 1912. In that
year was founded a magazine for the sole purpose of helping poems into the world; in that
year was published an anthology which meant
to become an annual, though, as it happened, another annual by another editor took its place the
year following. The real poetical event of 1912,
however, was the appearance in *The Lyric Year,*
tentative anthology, of the first outstanding poem
by Edna St. Vincent Millay. Who that then had
any taste of which he can now be proud but remembers the discovery, among the numerous failures and very innumerous successes which made
up the volume, of *Renascence,* by a girl of twenty
whose name none but her friends and a lucky
critic or two had heard? After wading through

tens and dozens of rhetorical strophes and moral stanzas, it was like suddenly finding wings to come upon these lines:

> "All I could see from where I stood
> Was three long mountains and a wood;
> I turned and looked another way,
> And saw three islands in a bay.
> So with my eyes I traced the line
> Of the horizon, thin and fine,
> Straight around till I was come
> Back to where I'd started from;
> And all I saw from where I stood
> Was three long mountains and a wood."

The diction was so plain, the arrangement so obvious, that the magic of the opening seemed a mystery; and yet the lift and turn of these verses were magical, as if a lark had taken to the air out of a dreary patch of stubble.

Nor did the poem falter as it went on. If it had the movement of a bird's flight, so had it the ease of a bird's song. The poet of this lucid voice had gone through a radiant experience. She had, she said with mystical directness, felt that she could touch the horizon, and found that she could touch the sky. Then infinity had settled down upon her till she could hear

> "The ticking of Eternity."

YOUTH AND WINGS

The universe pressed close and crushed her, oppressing her with omniscience and omnisentience; all sin, all remorse, all suffering, all punishment, all pity poured into her, torturing her. The weight drove her into the cool earth, where she lay buried, but happy, under the falling rain.

> "The rain, I said, is kind to come
> And speak to me in my new home.
> I would I were alive again
> To kiss the fingers of the rain,
> To drink into my eyes the shine
> Of every slanting silver line."

Suddenly came over her the terrible memory of the "multi-colored, multiform, beloved" beauty she had lost by this comfortable death. She burst into a prayer so potent that the responding rain, gathering in a black wave, opened the earth above her and set her free.

> "Ah! Up then from the ground sprang I
> And hailed the earth with such a cry
> As is not heard save from a man
> Who has been dead, and lives again.
> About the trees my arms I wound;
> Like one gone mad I hugged the ground;
> I raised my quivering arms on high;
> I laughed and laughed into the sky."

Whereupon, somewhat quaintly, she moralized her experience with the pride of youth finally arrived at full stature in the world.

> "The heart can push the sea and land
>   Farther away on either hand;
>   The soul can split the sky in two,
>   And let the face of God shine through.
>   But East and West will pinch the heart
>   That cannot keep them pushed apart;
>   And he whose soul is flat—the sky
>   Will cave in on him by and by."

Renascence, one of the loveliest of American poems, was an adventure, not an allegory, but it sounds almost allegorical because of the way it interpreted and distilled the temper which, after a long drought, was coming into American verse. Youth was discovering a new world, or thought it was. It had taken upon itself burdens of speculation, of responsibility, and had sunk under the weight. Now, on fire with beauty, it returned to joy and song.

2

Other things than joy and song, however, cut across the track of this little renaissance. There was a war. Youth—at least that part of it which makes poems—went out to fight, first with passion for the cause and then with contempt for the dotards who had botched and bungled. Gray Tyrtæuses might drone that here was a good war designed to end war, but youth meantime saw that it was dying in hordes and tried to snatch what ecstasy it could before the time should come when there would be no more ecstasy. Boys and girls who would otherwise have followed the smooth paths of their elders now questioned them and turned aside into different paths of life. Young men and maidens who would otherwise have expected little of love for years to come now demanded all that love offers, and demanded it immediately for fear it might come too late. The planet was reeling, or looked to be; all the settled orders were straining and breaking. Amid the hurly-burly of argument and challenge and recrimination a lyric had a good chance to be unheard; yet it was a lyrical hour, as it always is when the poet sees himself surrounded by swift moments hurrying to an end. Some sense of this in the air, even amid the hurly-burly, gave to the youth of the time that rash, impatient, wild ardor and insolence and cynicism which followed in such fleet succession, growing sharper as the war which was to have been good turned into the peace which was bound to be bad.

Miss Millay's *Aria da Capo*, like *Renascence*, has an allegorical sound, because it lays its finger so surely upon the mad sickness of the race during those futile years. The little play, now dainty with artifice and now racy with slang and satire, opens with Columbine and Pierrot skylarking in their pretty fashion, using, however, words with two sharp edges to each of them. But they are driven from the stage by tragedy, which sets the friendly shepherds Thyrsis and Corydon to playing a scene in which they divide their mimic field with colored ribbons, which they call a wall, find one of them mimic water on his side and the other mimic jewels, move on to a conflict which they did not mean or want and which they see is hardly so much reality as senseless acting, and in the end kill each other across the barrier, dying in each other's arms. Back come Pierrot and Columbine to resume, only a little disturbed by the dead bodies lying under their feet, the happy farce. Love among the ruins! Butterflies above the battle! Such folly as had been acted by the nations, the play hints, belongs rather to the painted theater than to the solid earth. There is not enough wisdom to understand it; there are not enough tears to bewail it. It may be better to frolic and forget.

3

The decade since the little renaissance began has created a kind of symbol for this irresponsible mood in the more or less mythical Greenwich Village, where, according to the popular legend, art and mirth flourish without a care, far from the stupid duties of human life. No one so well as Miss Millay has spoken with the accents credited to the village.

> "My candle burns at both ends;
> It will not last the night;
> But ah, my foes, and oh, my friends—
> It gives a lovely light!"

Thus she commences in *A Few Figs from Thistles*. And she continues with impish songs and rakish ballads and sonnets which laugh at the love which throbs through them. Suckling was not more insouciant than she is in *Thursday:*

> "And if I loved you Wednesday,
> Well, what is that to you?
> I do not love you Thursday—
> So much is true.

And why you come complaining
Is more than I can see.
I loved you Wednesday—yes—but what
Is that to me?"

With what a friendliness for wild souls she tells the story of the singing woman "Whose mother was a leprechaun, whose father was a friar."

"In through the bushes, on any foggy day,
My Da would come a-swishing of the drops away,
With a prayer for my death and a groan for my birth,
A-mumbling of his beads for all that he was worth.

And there sit my Ma, her knees beneath her chin,
A-looking in his face and a-drinking of it in,
And a-marking in the moss some funny little saying
That would mean just the opposite of all that he was
        praying!

He taught me the holy-talk of Vesper and of Matin,
He heard me my Greek and he heard me my Latin,
He blessed me and crossed me to keep my soul from
        evil,
And we watched him out of sight, and we conjured up
        the devil!

Oh, the things I haven't seen and the things I haven't
        known,
What with hedges and ditches till after I was grown,

[112]

And yanked both ways by my mother and my father,
With a 'Which would you better?' and a 'Which would
    you rather?'

With him for a sire and her for a dam,
What should I be but just what I am?"

Speaking in this manner, Greenwich Village
seems a long way from the village of Concord,
heart of the old tradition, even though Hawthorne loved a faun when he met one, and
Thoreau was something of a faun himself. In
the classic village any such mixture as this of
leprechaun and friar would have been kept as
close a secret as possible, and conscience would
have been set to the work of driving the
leprechaun taint out. In Greenwich Village the
friar is made to look a little comical, especially
to the mother and daughter who conspire to have
their fling behind his back.

4

This tincture of diablerie appears again and
again in Miss Millay's verse, perhaps most of all
in the candor with which she talks of love. She
has put by the mask under which other poets
who were women, apparently afraid for the repu-

tation of their sex, have spoken as if they were men. She has put by the posture of fidelity which women in poetry have been expected to assume. She speaks with the voice of women who, like men, are thrilled by the beauty of their lovers and are stung by desire; who know, however, that love does not always vibrate at its first high pitch, and so, too faithful to love to insist upon clinging to what has become half-love merely, let go without desperation. A woman may be fickle for fun, Miss Millay suggests in various poems wherein this or that girl teases her lover with the threat to leave him or the claim that she has forgotten him; but so may a woman show wisdom by admitting the variability and transcience of love, as in this crystal sonnet:

"I know I am but summer to your heart,
  And not the full four seasons of the year;
  And you must welcome from another part
  Such noble moods as are not mine, my dear.
  No gracious weight of golden fruits to sell
  Have I, nor any wise and wintry thing;
  And I have loved you all too long and well
  To carry still the high sweet breast of spring.
  Wherefore I say: O love, as summer goes,
  I must be gone, steal forth with silent drums,
  That you may hail anew the bird and rose
  When I come back to you, as summer comes.

Else will you seek, at some not distant time,
Even your summer in another clime."

What sets Miss Millay's love-poems apart
from almost all those written in English by
women is the full pulse which, in spite of their
gay impudence, beats through them. She does
not speak in the name of forlorn maidens or of
wives bereft, but in the name of women who dare
to take love at the flood, if it offers, and who
later, if it has passed, remember with exultation
that they had what no coward could have had.
Conscience does not trouble them, nor any serious
division in their natures. No one of them weeps
because she has been a wanton, no one of them
because she has been betrayed. Rarely since
Sappho has a woman voicéd such delight in a
lover's beauty as this:

"What's this of death, from you who never will die?
 Think you the wrist that fashioned you in clay,
 The thumb that set the hollow just that way
 In your full throat and lidded the long eye
 So roundly from the forehead, will let lie
 Broken, forgotten, under foot some day
 Your unimpeachable body, and so slay
 The work he had been most remembered by?"

Rarely since Sappho has a woman written as
outspokenly as this.

[115]

"What lips my lips have kissed, and where, and why,
I have forgotten, and what arms have lain
Under my head till morning; but the rain
Is full of ghosts to-night, that tap and sigh
Upon the glass and listen for reply;
And in my heart there stirs a quiet pain
For unremembered lads that not again
Will turn to me at midnight with a cry."

In passages like these Miss Millay has given body and vesture to a sense of equality in love; to the demand by women that they be allowed to enter the world of adventure and experiment in love which men have long inhabited. But Miss Millay does not, like any feminist, argue for that equality. She takes it for granted, exhibits it in action, and turns it into beauty.

5

Beauty, not argument, is, after all, Miss Millay's concern and goal. She can be somewhat metaphysical about it, as in her contention that

"Euclid alone has looked on Beauty bare.
Let all who prate of Beauty hold their peace,
And lay them prone upon the earth and cease
To ponder on themselves, the while they stare
At nothing, intricately drawn nowhere
In shapes of shifting lineage."

For the most part, however, she stands with those who love life and persons too wholly to spend much passion upon anything abstract. She loves the special countenance of every season, the hot light of the sun, gardens of flowers with old, fragrant names, the salt smell of the sea along her native Maine coast, the sound of sheep-bells and dripping eaves and the unheard sound of city trees, the homely facts of houses in which men and women live, tales of quick deeds and eager heroisms, the cool, kind love of young girls for one another, the color of words, the beat of rhythm. The shining clarity of her style does not permit her to work the things she finds beautiful into tapestried verse; she will not ask a song to carry more than it can carry on the easiest wings; but in all her graver songs and sonnets she serves beauty in one way or another. Now she affirms her absolute loyalty to beauty; now she hunts it out in unexpected places; most frequently of all she buries it with some of the most exquisite dirges of her time.

These returning dirges and elegies and epitaphs are as much the natural speech of Miss Millay as is her insolence of joy in the visible and tangible world. Like all those who most love life and beauty, she understands that both are brief and mortal. They take her round and round in a passionate circle: because she loves them so ardently she knows they cannot last, and because she knows they cannot last she loves them the more ardently while they do. Dispositions such as hers give themselves to joy when their vitality is at its peaks; in their lower hours they weep over the graves of loveliness which are bound to crowd their courses. Having a high heart and a proud creed, Miss Millay leaves unwept some graves which other poets and most people water abundantly, but she is stabbed by the essential tragedy and pity of death. Thus she expresses the tragic powerlessness of those who live to hold those who die:

> "Nor shall my love avail you in your hour.
> In spite of all my love, you will arise
> Upon that day and wander down the air
> Obscurely as the unattended flower,
> It mattering not how beautiful you were,
> Or how belovèd above all else that dies."

Thus she expresses the pitiful knowledge which the living have that they cannot help the dead:

> "Be to her, Persephone,
> All the things I might not be;
> Take her head upon your knee.

YOUTH AND WINGS

> She that was so proud and wild,
> Flippant, arrogant and free,
> She that had no need of me,
> Is a little lonely child
> Lost in Hell,—Persephone,
> Take her head upon your knee;
> Say to her, 'My dear, my dear,
> It is not so dreadful here.' "

Are these only the accents of a minor poet, crying over withered roses and melted snows? Very rarely do minor poets strike such moving chords upon such universal strings. Still more rarely do merely minor poets have so much power over tragedy and pity, and yet in other hours have equal power over fire and laughter.

SMARTNESS AND LIGHT

H. L. Mencken

THE democratic dogma has had its critics in
America ever since the priests and magis-
trates of the first colonies began to note the restive
currents which stirred among their people.   Critics of the same temper roared at the Revolution,
and lost.   During the probationary years of the
republic there were Federalists, and then Whigs,
and eventually Republicans, to say nothing of
Bourbons of different varieties from time to time.
Most of these skeptic voices have been merely
political, but not all.   Poe, for instance, was a
poet, concerned with art and beauty, and a critic
who spread death among the idols of popular
taste.   H. L. Mencken is a wit, concerned less
with art or beauty than with the manners of
his nation, who aims his wrath at the very heart
of democracy, announces that the system is no
less a nuisance than a failure, and proclaims the

empire of excellence. Like Poe, he uses every
critical method except that of mercy, and, like
Poe, he wins applause at every death he deals.
He could not win this if there were not an alert
minority which delights in the victories of criticism over commonplace.

2

Mr. Mencken, at whom academic circles still
cock a frigid or a timid eye, grows steadily more
significant. Before the war, of which he says
that he neither advised nor approved it, he was a
useful conduit leading to the republic from Shaw
and Nietzsche and Ibsen. The war played into
his hands, it begins to look, as into those of
hardly any other literary American. Heretofore, to change the figure, he had been but an in-
tern in the hospital of his American kind, satisfied with an occasional run in the ambulance, an
occasional appendix to cut out, an occasional
skull to help trepan. Now he was suddenly invited to apply diagnosis, surgery, or the lethal
chamber in such a range of cases as no native
satirist had ever been allowed to practise on. He
found hundreds of politicians palsied with in-
competence, thousands of journalists and educa-

tors and preachers flatulent with prophecy, millions of patriots dropsical with sentimentalism. He found idealists who had delusions of grandeur, scholars who suffered from obsessions of hatred, business men who had been shell-shocked out of all self-control, women whose long-repressed instincts burst into frenzies of cruelty. He found, what seemed to him the source and cause of all these maladies, the plain people turned into a vast standard mass, now dumb and snuffling like a flock of sheep, now loud and savage like a pack of wolves. All the folly which overwhelmed him had, to his eyes, the symptoms of having risen from the body of democracy. No wonder, given his conception of life, that he should have laid aside his scalpel and have taken to the jolly bludgeon as the only tool he needed. No wonder, given the consequences of the madness he observed, that he should finally have declared the worst result of the war to be the fact that so many Americans survived it.

The wonder is, rather, that Mr. Mencken should have waked so many echoes among his countrymen. No other contemporary critic is so well known in the colleges. No other is so influential among the latest generation of boys and girls of letters. Substantial citizens and sound students who cannot agree with a half or a quarter of what he says, nevertheless delight in the burly way in which he says it and find themselves agreeing with more than they thought they could. He has endowed the decade with a whole glossary of words which breathe contempt for its imbecilities. It is in part because his voice is the least uncertain of all the critic voices that he is so clearly heard; but it is also in part because there was among Americans already a strong vein of discontent with democracy which needed only to be tapped to send forth gushers of criticism and ridicule. Idealism and optimism had been orthodox too long for their own health; suspicion had been gathering under the surface of the national temper. The war, by straining idealism to the point of reaction and optimism to the point of collapse, had considerably discredited both of them. The young and the irresponsible, looking at the mess the mature and the responsible had made of human life on the planet, lost what respect they had and broke out of bounds. Irreverence for institutions and ribald laughter for respectability and a hard directness of speech succeeded the older modes. And when the dispersed thousands who felt this new spirit cast about for a spokesman, they rapidly realized that in Mr. Mencken the hour had found its man.

3

What first attracted them was pretty certainly his impudence, as it attracts most readers to him at first. He is as brash as a sophomore is supposed to be. He has never heard of a head too sacred to be smitten. That something is taboo merely makes him want to try it once. He walks briskly into shrines and takes a cheerful turn through cemeteries. Here is what Mr. Mencken says of Lincoln's Gettysburg address, before which hardly an American has ever ventured to lift his voice unless he lifted it to a hymn: "It is eloquence brought to a pellucid and almost child-like perfection—the highest emotion reduced to one graceful and irresistible gesture. . . . But let us not forget that it is oratory, not logic; beauty, not sense. . . . The doctrine is simply this: that the Union soldiers who died at Gettysburg sacrificed their lives to the cause of self-determination—'that government of the people, by the people, for the people,' should not perish from the earth. It is difficult to imagine

anything more untrue. The Union soldiers in
that battle actually fought against self-determination; it was the Confederates who fought
for the right of their people to govern themselves.
. . . The Confederates went into the battle an
absolutely free people; they came out with their
freedom subject to the supervision and vote of
the rest of the country—and for nearly twenty
years that vote was so effective that they enjoyed
scarcely any freedom at all. Am I the first
American to note the fundamental nonsensicality
of the Gettysburg address? If so, I plead my
aesthetic joy in it in amelioration of the sac-
rilege."

His final sentence is, it may be said, much the
kind of impudence which led this critic in an
earlier book to call an archbishop "a Christian
ecclesiastic of a rank superior to that attained by
Christ." Both comments at least reveal a keen
pleasure in the saying of sharp things. But in
the whole comment upon Lincoln there is a
larger sagacity which grows upon Mr. Mencken
as he widens his inquiries and leaves mere witti-
cism behind him. Those whom he first attracts
by his impudence he holds by his sagacity. He
may play upon the saxophone with the gesticula-
tions of jazz, but he knows many important har-

monies and he constantly brings them into his performance. Regarding theology, politics, philosophy, law, medicine, art, business, morals, character, language, he has said some of the shrewdest things in his American generation. Not all are new, not all are true, but they proceed from a singularly powerful intelligence expressing itself in a singularly untrammeled speech. It happens to be a tory intelligence, impatient of whatever is untried, unimpressed by the bombastic, the heroic, the altruistic, scornful of the unsophisticated; an intelligence which holds that the vast majority of men are supine; that those who are not supine are foolish; that those who are not foolish are knavish; and that the few who have brains or virtues must stand together or they will be smothered in the mass. It happens also to be radical intelligence, cutting away excrescences of verbiage, challenging sluggish habits of thought, daring to drive through morasses of emotion to the solid ground of sense beyond, carrying the guidon of reason into desperate breaches. Tory or radical, this intelligence has a reach and thrust which make it noticeable, no matter of what persuasion its observers may at any moment be.

Such an intelligence, however, unaided by

other qualities, could never have got Mr. Mencken his audience. Instead of being astringent, as his doctrine might have made him, he is amazingly full of the sap of life and comedy. Not since Poe has an American critic taken such a fling or enjoyed it more. The motive of criticism, he maintains, "is not the motive of the pedagogue, but the motive of the artist. It is no more and no less than the simple desire to function freely and beautifully, to give outward and objective form to ideas that bubble inwardly and have a fascinating lure in them, to get rid of them dramatically and make an articulate noise in the world. . . . It is the pressing yearning of every man who has ideas in him to empty them upon the world, to hammer them into plausible and ingratiating shapes, to compel the attention and respect of his equals, to lord it over his inferiors." Yet even this exciting conception of the art of criticism had to be joined with a particular endowment if Mr. Mencken was to be the personage he is. That endowment is gusto, and gusto he possesses in a degree which no one of his contemporaries can rival. In a decade of which too many of the critics have dyspepsia, Mr. Mencken, as he might say, "goes the whole hog."

There comes to mind a curious parallel with
Whitman, drunk with joy in the huge spectacle
of his continent filled with his countrymen. Sitting in New York or Camden, he sent his imagination out over the land, across all its mountains
and prairies, along all its rivers, into all its cities,
among all its citizens at their occupations. He
accepted all, he rejected nothing, because his affection was great enough to embrace the entire
republic. His long panoramas, his crowded
categories, are evidence that he gloated over the
details of American life as a lover gloats over
the charms of his mistress or a mother over the
merits of her baby. So, in his different fashion,
Mr. Mencken gloats over the follies of the republic. But is his fashion so different from
Whitman's as it appears at first glance? His intellectual position compels him to see a side
which Whitman overlooked. What to Whitman
seemed a splendid turbulence, to Mr. Mencken
seems a headless swirl. What to Whitman
seemed a noble cohesiveness, seems to Mr.
Mencken a herd-like conventionality. What to
Whitman seemed a hopeful newness, seems to Mr.
Mencken a hopeless rawness. Yet the satirist
no less than the poet revels in the gaudy spectacle. "The United States, to my eye," Mr.

Mencken explicitly says, "is incomparably the greatest show on earth. It is a show which avoids diligently all the kinds of clowning which tire me most quickly—for example, royal ceremonials, the tedious hocus-pocus of *haut politique*, the taking of politics seriously—and lays chief stress upon the kinds which delight me unceasingly—for example, the ribald combats of demagogues, the exquisitely ingenious operations of master rogues, the pursuit of witches and heretics, the desperate struggles of inferior men to claw their way into Heaven. We have clowns in constant practice among us who are as far above the clowns of any other great state as a Jack Dempsey is above a paralytic—and not a few dozens or score of them, but whole droves and herds. Human enterprises which, in all other Christian countries, are resigned despairingly to an incurable dullness—things that seem devoid of exhilarating amusement by their very nature—are here lifted to such vast heights of buffoonery that contemplating them strains the midriff almost to breaking."

4

Is Mr. Mencken, then, an enemy of his people? "Here I stand," he contends, "unshaken and undespairing, a loyal and devoted Americano, even a chauvinist, paying taxes without complaint, obeying all laws that are physiologically obeyable, accepting all the searching duties and responsibilities of citizenship unprotestingly, investing the sparse usufructs of my miserable toil in the obligations of the nation, avoiding all commerce with men sworn to overthrow the government, contributing my mite toward the glory of the national arts and science, spurning all lures (and even all invitations) to go out and stay out . . . here am I, contentedly and even smugly basking beneath the Stars and Stripes, a better citizen, I daresay, and certainly a less murmurous and exigent one, than thousands who put the Hon. Warren Gamaliel Harding beside Friedrich Barbarossa and Charlemagne, and hold the Supreme Court to be directly inspired by the Holy Spirit, and belong ardently to every Rotary Club, Ku Klux Klan, and Anti-Saloon League, and choke with emotion when the band plays the 'Star-Spangled Banner,' and believe with the faith of little children that one of Our Boys, taken at random, could dispose in a fair fight of ten Englishmen, twenty Germans, thirty Frogs, forty Wops, fifty Japs, or a hundred Bolsheviki." Whitman, with whatever other tones or arguments, never exhibited his essential Americanism more convincingly. Have Americans no speech but praise? Have they no song but rhapsody?

The truth of the matter is, Mr. Mencken is one of the most American things we have. Both his art and his success spring from the gusto which draws him to the comic aspects of the life around him—draws him with as great an eagerness as if he accepted all he saw and acclaimed it. To read him, even while dissenting from his doctrine on every page, is to gasp and whoop with recognition. Thus, for instance, he illustrates "Eminence," without a word of commentary: "The leading Methodist layman of Pottawattamie county, Iowa. . . . The man who won the limerick contest conducted by the Toomsboro, Ga., *Banner*. . . . The President of the Johann Sebastian Bach *Bauverein* of Highlandtown, Md. . . . The girl who sold the most Liberty Bonds in Duquesne, Pa. . . . The man who owns the best bull in Coosa County, Ala. . . . The oldest subscriber to the Raleigh, N. C., *News and Observer*. . . . The author of the ode read at the unveiling of the monument to General Robert E. Lee at Valdosta, Ga. . . . The old lady in Wahoo, Neb., who has read the Bible 38 times. . . .

The professor of chemistry, Greek, rhetoric, and piano at the Texas Christian University, Fort Worth, Tex. . . . The leading dramatic critic of Pittsburgh. . . . The night watchman in Penn Yan, N. Y., who once shook hands with Chester A. Arthur"—and on and on with Rabelaisian fecundity. Nothing petty, nothing absurd, nothing grotesque, nothing racy of the soil, seems to have escaped Mr. Mencken's terrible eye. Though he has not traveled very widely in the United States, he knows the map as well as any continental drummer. Though he has taken only a journalist's hand in actual politics, he is virtually the first to hoot at any new political asininity. As if with a hundred newspapers and a hundred clubs for his whispering gallery, he appears to have heard every secret and every scandal. Nor does he content himself with random citation of what he hits upon. He hoards them and makes treatises. With George Jean Nathan, his dapper David, this rugged Jonathan has collected nearly a thousand vulgar beliefs in *An American Credo;* by himself he has composed a large first and a huge second edition of *The American Language.* He has, in short, the range of a journalist, the verve of a comic poet, the patience of a savant. Among American humorists no one but Mark Twain has had more "body" to his art than Mr. Mencken.

5

Poe, Whitman, Mark Twain—are they unexpected companions for a former editor of the *Smart Set?* Perhaps; and yet Mr. Mencken, laying aside to some extent the waggish elements in his constitution, begins to have the stature of an important man of letters. Unlike Poe, he has in him nothing of the poet and he has written nonsense about poetry. Unlike Whitman, he has not deeply studied the common man at first hand and he dismisses such persons with the insolence of a city wit. Unlike Mark Twain, he despises the miserable race of man without, like Mark Twain, also pitying it. What Mr. Mencken most conspicuously lacks, indeed, is the mood of pity, an emotion which the greatest satirists have all exhibited now or then. Even Swift, as indisposed to forgive a fool as Mr. Mencken is, occasionally let fall a glance of compassion upon folly. This is the particular penalty of smartness: though it may have plenty of light, it fears, even for a moment, to be sweet. Embar-rassed in the presence of nothing else, it is embarrassed in the presence of ungirt emotions. Far from suffering fools gladly, it finds it difficult to overlook the dash of folly which appears in enthusiasm and heroism. Any habitual addiction to smartness makes almost impossible that highest quality of the mind, magnanimity. Mr. Mencken is but rarely magnanimous. It seems significant that he, passionately devoted as he is to music, so often misses the finer tones of eloquence when, as in poetry or prophecy, they are attended by expressed ideas which his reason challenges. Unless he can take his music "straight," he suspects it. The virtue of his quality of suspicion is that it helps him to see through things; its vice is that it frequently keeps him from seeing round them.

At the same time, however, Mr. Mencken is an utter stranger to parsimonious or ungenerous impulses. No one takes a trouncing more cheerfully than he; no one holds out a quicker hand of encouragement to any promising beginner in literature or scholarship. The stupidity against which he wages his hilarious war is the stupidity which, unaware of its defects, has first sought to shackle the children of light. It is chiefly at sight of such attempts that his indignation rises and that he rushes forth armed with a bagpipe, a slapstick, a shillalah, a pitchfork, a butcher's cleaver, a Browning rifle, a lusty arm, and an undaunted heart. What fun, then! Seeing that the feast of fools has still its uses, he elects himself boy-bishop, gathers a horde of revelers about him, and burlesques the universe. Of course he profanes the mysteries, but the laughter with which he does it and the laughter which he arouses among the by-standers have the effect of clearing the packed atmosphere. When the saturnalia ends, sense settles down again with renewed authority. If it is a service to Mr. Mencken's country for him to be so often right in his quarrels and to bring down with his merry bullets so many giant imbecilities, even though with his barrage he not seldom slays some honest and charming idealism; so also it is a service to his country for him, even while he is vexing a few of the judicious with his excess of smartness, to enrich the nation with such a powerful stream of humor as no other American is now playing upon the times.

FLAME AND SLAG

Carl Sandburg

THE older stocks of the United States have in their imaginations one picture of the country and its inhabitants; the newer stocks have another. In the first there is the persistent image of the pioneer advancing from the seaboard, by forest trail and waterway, across rich prairie and naked plain, contending mightily, romantically, victoriously with aboriginal men and beasts, in the end settling peacefully down in farm, village, or thriving city to enjoy the Canaan he has thus won for himself and his children's children. The air of this picture is fresh and pure, the earth green with grass, the roads fouled with nothing worse than mud; food may be had for the taking, shelter for the building, land for the seeking. If there are hardships, they are relatively brief, yielding to enterprise and thrift in a decade or two at most. If there are ugly aspects, they are largely unpreventable, like frontier violence or ignorance, and they yield to solid contentment and popular enlightenment. Ultimately these stocks inherit the earth, in the picture, though increasingly their descendants look with irritation and some anger upon the later stocks who are arriving among them and beside them. The new-comers, beginning anew the old process, have other images for it. Their pioneer is set down in shop or mill or mine, herded with others of his race in a slum, exploited at every turn by the lucky older stocks, forced to carry the double burden of making his way in a hostile world and of remaking himself into the pattern of man which that world requires. He breathes air which is black with smoke or smutted with the grime of cities. He finds no welcoming land for his house or garden. Wherever he turns, others have been there before him and erected obstacles more difficult or at least more complicated than the first settlers had to level in their war with stubborn nature. He has not been long enough on the continent to cherish that epic sense of the American past which even the dullest members of the older stocks have picked up in some degree or other from the little history they know; he is sustained, instead, by that sense of a radiant American future which helped draw him from his native soil. He rarely has the easy humor which has arisen in part from the free and open lives of the older stocks; he has, instead, the darker irony which springs from his discovery of the contrast between the vision which drew him hither and the facts which awaited him. By his hopefulness he is made more naïve, by his irony more sophisticated than the average older American.

2

Carl Sandburg, a genius, not an average man, speaks out of the sentiments of the new order of Americans. The son of a Swedish immigrant, he himself in his youth belonged to the ranks of unskilled labor, drifting about the Middle West at odd jobs and into a volunteer company as a private during the war with Spain. His subsequent career in college and in journalism but gave him words for emotions which had been beating within him in his inarticulate years. He too, like the typical immigrant pioneer, flames with the future, though in Mr. Sandburg the flame leaps higher than it has done in any other poet of his order. With what fervor, in *Prayers of Steel,* he voices the aspiration not only of steel but of men to give themselves to a great cause:

"Lay me on an anvil, O God.
  Beat me and hammer me into a crowbar.
  Let me pry loose old walls.
  Let me lift and loosen old foundations.
  Lay me on an anvil, O God.
  Beat me and hammer me into a steel spike.
  Drive me into the girders that hold a skyscraper to-
      gether.
  Take red-hot rivets and fasten me into the central
      girders.
  Let me be the great nail holding a skyscraper through
      blue nights into white stars."

A poet of the older order might have put some such prayer into the mouth of a plow or of an ax or of a tree or of a stone, eager each of them to be used at no matter what cost to themselves; for a poet of the new order steel has taken the place of these things among the images of ardor and devotion. The immigrants—how many of them!—live by steel, within sight of it melting in furnaces, within sound of it clanging into place in structures that crowd the earth and shut out the sun. They have found that steel, long symbol for a warrior, may be symbol as well for a martyr or a saint.

Yet Mr. Sandburg, thus close to the world of steel and smoke around him, is not buried in it, but sees it under the long light of irony, as in the poem which he slyly calls *Limited:*

"I am riding on a limited express, one of the crack
      trains of the nation.
  Hurtling across the prairie into blue haze and dark air
      go fifteen all-steel coaches holding a thousand
      people.
  (All the coaches shall be scrap and rust and all the
      men and women laughing in the diners and sleep-
      ers shall pass to ashes.)
  I ask a man in the smoker where he is going and he
      answers: 'Omaha.' "

With infinite destiny ahead of him, the man in the smoker, the poet learns, sees no further than one undistinguished town. The artist in Mr. Sandburg, thus viewing the life of an industrial society around him, employs it passionately for his art; the thinker, no less than in any simpler age, understands that the things which seem most solid among the works of man will flow into other forms, as clouds and mountains do, and that nothing holds the long span of human time together but the flexible links of change running through the generations.

From this irony, mated with this rapture, springs the tenderness which barely misses being Mr. Sandburg's most distinctive trait. He writes exquisitely of children, in the brooding, reverent, whimsical tone of a father speaking to his little daughters, touched by the coolness in them, aware of the fire there, thinking how soon both shall do their work and go:

"There are dreams in your eyes, Helga.
 Tall reaches of wind sweep the clear blue.
 The winter is young yet, so young.
 Only a little cupful of winter has touched your lips."

So abundant is his tenderness for children that he has taken the trouble to create, in his *Rootabaga* stories, a sort of nonsense idiom, based upon the America vernacular, in which to tell stories to children about the world which he enters when he talks to them—a roguish, mad, grotesque, edifying world where all the fancies of childhood come to life and frolic with the gestures of slang. He writes tenderly of old people remembering, of fragile souls driven into paths too steep for them, of the hulks of broken men, of the pity that lies near the heart of friendship and love, near the sense of beauty, near the willingness to forgive life for being no better than it is because it is as good as it is. Among all the recent American poets Mr. Sandburg speaks most naturally with the accents of pity.

3

Pity, indeed, carries him now and then to the point of bathos, as in that often cited line in *Chicago Poems* in which he makes Truth boast:

"I dabble in the blood and guts of the terrible."

Or, rather, pity for many things ordinarily unconsidered or trodden under foot carries his sympathy to a point beyond the reach of his imagination, so that, as Whitman did before him, he runs into long lists of objects which he declares are beautiful or moving, but which, if they are so to him, are so to him only, for the reason that he has not an imaginative power over them sufficient to bring them into any universal language. To go back now, however, after seven years to Mr. Sandburg's first book of verse is to observe how much which seemed unassimilated then in his poetry now seems to fit into the general pattern, as it fits into the pattern of the poetic idiom of the century. Not for many years can Chicago occur to the mind of any reader of poetry without some reminiscence, direct or indirect, of the loud words with which its chief poet has saluted or characterized it:

"Hog Butcher for the World,
 Tool Maker, Stacker of Wheat,
 Player with Railroads and the Nation's Freight Handler;
 Stormy, husky, brawling,
 City of the Big Shoulders: . . .
 Come and show me another city with lifted head singing
     so proud to be alive and coarse and strong and
     cunning.
 Flinging magnetic curses amid the toil of piling job on
     job, here is a tall bold slugger set vivid against the
     little soft cities; . . .
 Laughing even as an ignorant fighter laughs who has
     never lost a battle,
 Bragging and laughing that under his wrist is the pulse,
     and under his ribs the heart of the people,
                    Laughing!"

"Go to it and remember this city fished from its depths
     a text: 'independent as a hog on ice.'
 Venice is a dream of soft waters, Vienna and Bagdad
     recollections of dark spears and wild turbans;
     Paris is a thought in Monet gray on scabbards, fab-
     rics, façades; London is a fact in a fog filled with
     the moaning of transatlantic whistles; Berlin sits

amid white scrubbed quadrangles and torn arith-
metics and testaments; Moscow brandishes a flag
and repeats a dance figure of a man who walks
like a bear.

Chicago fished from its depths a text: 'Independent
as a hog on ice.' "

Chicago, the windy, insolent city, was of all
themes the one most likely to excite this poet
whom it has helped to shape. He found in it a
spectacle grandiose enough for his taste, yet not
enough in the grand style, since it lacks the tra-
ditional and the ceremonial, to amuse the satirist
in him. He found, as he goes on finding, the
city enormous, unformed, moving in a direction
not yet determined, but obviously started on a
long road with momentum sufficient to take it almost any distance. Here innumerable races
have come together, immigrant stocks, to hack
out their own new Canaan on their own new
model. If their task is a hard one, at least they
do not have the task of destroying elaborate
hierarchies, for Chicago is still, in comparison
with New York or with European or Asiatic cities, the village of villages, sprawling and neighborly, innocent of the compact organization of
older societies. Here common men and common

women and common children swirl as in Mr.
Sandburg's vision of life, modestly attending to
their business, robustly elbowing their way to
their desires. What for another poet might be
distasteful in the noise and disorder of Chicago
is for Mr. Sandburg inspiriting, because it seems
to him the symptom of power and freedom.
For power and freedom to him are most impressive in their shirt-sleeves. He is not stirred by
the king or the bishop on his throne, by the
premier or the capitalist at his desk, by the general or the admiral at the head of disciplined
forces; these men to him are but pictures of
power, not power itself, because they merely
guide, and that at second hand, concerted energies which have already lost their prime vigor
in the process of being regimented. His imagination insists on turning to the raw materials of
existence, on being lifted by the sight of human
elements not yet civilized. Such materials and
elements he has found in unmatched bulk in his
stormy, husky, brawling city.

4

Mr. Sandburg's language ranges freely from
the fine, pure speech of his too few lyrics to the

boisterous vernacular with which he plays on the
trombone and the horse fiddle.   He can write as
hauntingly as in these lines from *Cornhuskers:*

"Bees and a honeycomb in the dried head of a horse in
a pasture corner—a skull in the tall grass and a
buzz and a buzz of the yellow honey-hunters.
And I ask no better a winding sheet (over the earth and
under the sun.)
Let the bees go honey-hunting with yellow blur of
wings in the dome of my head, in the rumbling,
singing arch of my skull.
Let there be wings and yellow dust and the drone of
dreams of honey—who loses and remembers?—who
keeps and forgets?
In a blue sheen of moon over the bones and under the
hanging honeycomb the bees come home and the
bees sleep."

He can write as curtly and sardonically as in
these lines from *Smoke and Steel:*

"Five geese deploy mysteriously.
Onward proudly with flagstaffs,
Hearses with silver bugles,
Bushels of plum-blossoms dropping
For ten mystic web-feet—
Each his own drum major,
Each charged with the honor
Of the ancient goose nation,
Each with a nose-length surpassing

[146]

FLAME AND SLAG

    The nose-length of rival nations.
    Somberly, slowly, unimpeachably,
    Five geese deploy, mysteriously."

He can explode in a guffaw of disgust at persons who seem to him to tangle the skeins of life:

"The work of a bricklayer goes to the blue.
  The knack of a mason outlasts a moon.
  The hand of a plasterer holds a room together.
  The land of a farmer wishes him back again.
    Singers of songs and dreamers of plays
    Build a house no wind blows over
  The lawyers—tell me why a hearse horse snickers haul-
    ing a lawyer's bones."

He was perhaps never more thoroughly himself as a poet than when, on the occasion of the burial of the Unknown Soldier, he disturbed the universal chorus of solemn eloquence with his terrible picture, in *And So To-day,* of a skeleton army riding down Pennsylvania Avenue, unseen by the official orators, and yet mocking them as they go about the rites.

"The honorable orators,
  Always the honorable orators,
  Buttoning the buttons on their prinz alberts,
  Pronouncing the syllables 'sac-ri-fice,'
  Juggling those bitter salt-soaked syllables—

Do they ever gag with hot ashes in their mouths?
Do their tongues shrivel with a pain of fire
Across those simple syllables 'sac-ri-fice?' "

To Mr. Sandburg the ceremony seemed a kind
of blasphemy. As he saw it, the "buck private"
thus chosen for symbolic honors had not died as
a symbol, but as an actual man, burned by dis-
ease or torn by gunshot, racked by the solitary
agony which goes with death in no matter what
cause. Nor was it certain that the unknown
soldier had loved or even approved this cause.
How, then, as long as there was this doubt, could
he be paid in the coin of this show? It meant
nothing to Mr. Sandburg to be told that the survivors had no other coin, and that they were
doing what they could to discharge their sense of
obligation. The dead man had belonged to the
primary material of human life. He had died
not while going about his own affairs of work or
'love but while doing what others had commanded
him to do for their sake as well as his. If now,
when his senses were stopped, they were smother-
ing him with words and roses, it was with roses
for them to smell, with words for them to hear.
At such a spectacle Mr. Sandburg could feel no
mood but a brooding, savage irony, and could
find no outlet but to burst forth in his rough,

[148]

powerful language, hooting lest he weep, reminding the mourners of the skeleton orator who stood
by, almost silent:

"And he had nothing to say, nothing easy—
He mentioned ten million men, mentioned them as having
    gone west, mentioned them as shoving up the daisies.
We could write it all on a postage stamp, what he said."

5

Mr. Sandburg has trouble as well as luck with
the raw materials of life which he handles and
with the raw materials of language which he
uses in handling them. Both his trouble and his
luck come from his unwillingness, possibly his
inability, to accept any help whatever. He will
not see with the majority, and thus take advantage of audiences already prepared to thrill him.
He will not touch customary themes, and thus
take advantage of the failures or successes of
other poets with those themes. He will not select
his language from among the tried and prosperous words of poetry, but insists on grabbing up
any or all words and hammering them into the
shape he chooses. The consequences of his
method are that he often strikes off sparks of a
peculiar vividness and that he often throws off
cinders of no vividness at all, much as their

weight may be. To go through his books is to stumble again and again upon heaps of slag, ore never quite melted or ore in some way burned past any use, spread about in a large disorder. Yet here and there from these piles of slag emerge objects of a strangely authentic beauty and grace and tenderness. And over the whole field, what hot, what blue flames leap and dance!

SALVATION WITH JAZZ

Vachel Lindsay

CHURCH and state in the United States are
allied at least to this degree: reforms and
revivals take lessons from each other. The
rhythm of each is the rhythm of crusade. When
souls or cities are to be saved, the tambourine
must be shaken, the trombone must disturb the
sky. The roots of the American revival go back
to Jonathan Edwards, that Peter the Hermit of
New England, who found his people sunk in the
dullness of prose and sought to lift them up and
draw them after him in a march upon the City of
God which he believed might be discovered, or
established, on their own soil. The roots of
American reform go back to the poets and orators
of the Revolution, who found their people accepting too tamely the smug rule of Great Britain,
and taught them to hope and work for a republic
of mankind which was to replace their ancient

[151]

form of government when they should have put forth efforts heroic enough to earn a republic. The Great Awakening and the Glorious Revolution thus early set the pace and called the dance which have continued ever since. Even when, as in many of its aspects, American life has become doggedly or venomously reactionary, the rhythm of crusade has kept on throbbing in the popular imagination. Theodore Roosevelt is but the archetype of countless strenuous Americans who, fired by a vision of civil excellence, start the bagpipes skirling and raise a rhythmic din among their warriors as they advance toward some high political goal. Billy Sunday is but the archetype of countless strenuous natives who, inflamed with a passion for the good old cause, hang bells upon their caps, set the tom-tom going, and sweep forward, or backward, to the pulse of jazz, to the roar of camp-followers drunk with the pious opportunity.

2

Vachel Lindsay emerged from a plane of culture on which such enthusiasms flourish. He is, among recent American poets, the most impetuous enthusiast. Only he, among those recent American poets who are also important, has a record, which he avows, of membership in a more or less militant denomination, of admiration for foreign missionaries, of activities in the Young Men's Christian Association, of blows struck in behalf of the Anti-Saloon League. Other bards may see in prohibition a set of statutes against cakes and ale or an increase of tyranny deftly managed by clever lobbyists in the interests of a comfortable minority with stocks in its cellars; to Mr. Lindsay the prohibition movement is, or was, a gallant revolution against the sour and savage King Alcohol who has too long ruled the race. Others may see in Y.M.C.A. secretaries the least imaginative of those persons who believe that a Christian should be all things to all men, and may see in foreign missionaries the least imaginative of those persons who believe that God should be one thing to all men; to Mr. Lindsay such secretaries and missionaries are, or were, knights and paladins whose quarrels are just, whose conquests are beneficent, because they uphold and extend the healing hands of Christ. Others may see in the Campbellites an undistinguished, though aggressive, village sect with apostolic prejudices; to Mr. Lindsay the Disciples are the faithful legionaries of Alexander Campbell, the pioneer who proclaimed a millennium in the Western wilderness and set the feet of his companions and inheritors on the path which leads to a New Jerusalem.

Most of the poems in which Mr. Lindsay utters or hints at these opinions are early, and most of them are, as poems, trash. They are not, however, the whole story. They are merely items in his attempt to give his work a basis in the moods and in the rhythms of his native section. As a student of art in Chicago and in New York he was not entirely at home; he could not find a natural idiom to match his impulses. That idiom he eventually found in a language which expresses the mood of the local patriot in the rhythm of national vaudeville. He devised the terms "the new localism" and "the higher vaudeville" to give the authority of doctrine to his practice. Localism, of course, had long been one of the most potent forces in the country, particularly in Mr. Lindsay's Middle West. Town had striven with town to see which could sing its own praises loudest and so further its own aspirations by bringing in new inhabitants and larger business. The strife had encouraged all the natural tendencies toward optimism and complacency, and had developed the windy lingo of the booster until it had become perhaps the most customary oratory of the region. Here was something, Mr. Lindsay felt, to be translated into the worthier idiom of poetry. But he was a booster of a novel disposition. He wanted to see brought to his town of Springfield not more business but more beauty; not more inhabitants but more elevation of life.

This is what Mr. Lindsay himself undertook to do. He wandered in the South and East and got material for *A Handy Guide for Beggars*, full of counsel for such as find themselves choked by houses and bored by books, and so take to the open road of the poet and the vagabond. He wandered from Illinois to New Mexico and got material for *Adventures While Preaching the Gospel of Beauty,* that quaint, racy, joyful narrative of his experiences while he was about his singular evangelism. On both journeys he carried with him his *Rhymes to Be Traded for Bread,* got food and shelter by them, and scattered the seed of beauty on every kind of soil he met. The good he did to others it would be hard to estimate, but the good done to him by his adventures is unmistakable. He came back to Springfield fully developed as a poet. Hence-

forth he was to be contented to live in that inland
capital. He would voice its aspirations, he
would interpret its folk-ways, he would use its
dialect, he would snare its rhythms, he would
write words for the tunes which rang through its
sleepy head.

3

His creed was less original than his performance. There had been Americans before him
who had in mind to make Boston as memorable
as Athens, New York as memorable as Paris;
and other Americans who vowed to make Indianapolis as memorable as Boston, or San Francisco
as memorable as New York. A European,
standing beside a river, calls it liquid history;
an American, beside a river in his own land, sees
prophecy in it, and thinks what memories are
being cast upon its waters by the great deeds being done along its banks. All that was new in
Mr. Lindsay's passion was its special object and
method. He was the first to boost for beauty in
the common American language. In his earliest
notable poem, *General William Booth Enters Into
Heaven,* he took the theme of a revival sermon
and the rhythm of a revival hymn and achieved

the fruitful marriage of salvation with jazz. So much is national, but Mr. Lindsay gives his poem a touch of local color such as any medieval painter might have given it.

"Jesus come out from the court-house door,
Stretched his hands above the passing poor.
Booth saw not, but led his queer ones there,
Round and round the mighty court-house square."

The scene of the triumphant entry is Springfield, or some town like it; Mr. Lindsay had brought the drama of salvation home to his own neighbors.

After piety, patriotism. If Mr. Lindsay had seen poetic possibilities in the Salvation Army, so did he see them in the spectacle of countless motors streaming across the continent in a grandiose pageant. As a tramping evangelist in Kansas he had at first resented the proud speed of the automobiles dashing past him, but in time he lost his resentment in his fascination.

"I would not walk all alone till I die
Without some life-drunk horns going by."

Do the roaring engines and the raw horns disturb the peace of dreams? So does the march of life always disturb them. But dreams, after all, come back when the thunder of the procession dies. Meanwhile there is magnificence in the rush of so many motors, each one bearing a pennant with the name of the city from which it hails. In *The Santa Fe Trail: A Humoresque* Mr. Lindsay reels off the names of the cities in the manner of a train-caller in a railway station —reels them off till he is drunk with the motley syllables and in his exaltation sees the United States go by. Here he is even more native than in his poem on Booth, for Booth was an Englishman who arrived in a reasonably international paradise; but the flood of automobiles pouring across Kansas, perceived by a poet crusading for the new localism, and chanted in a manner based upon a train-caller's drone—this is home-grown, home-spun, home-measured, home-made.

Mr. Lindsay sought, however, to go still deeper into his soil. Springfield has Negroes among its citizens and has had race riots. To the superficial eye these particular Americans seem to give themselves to loose habits, hilarious amusements, fantastic religions. In the literary tradition they have regularly been regarded as mere comic figures or as pathetic victims of oppression. The higher vaudeville sees other aspects:

SALVATION WITH JAZZ

"Then I had religion, then I had a vision.
I could not turn from their revel in derision.
Then I saw the Congo, creeping through the black,
Cutting through the forest with a golden track."

These particular Americans are also Africans. The jungle is in their blood: loud colors, powerful odors, witchcraft, malign deities.   Mr. Lindsay, observing

"Fat black bucks in a wine-barrel room. . . .
Beat an empty barrel with the handle of a broom,"

hears behind them

"the boom of the blood-lust song
And a thigh-bone beating on a tin-pan gong."

Observing crap-shooters and cake-walkers at their irrepressible play, he sees a Negro fairy-land with gaudy revelers laughing at the witch-doctors who try to cow them with talk of Mumbo-Jumbo:

"Just then from the doorway, as fat as shotes,
Came the cake-walk princes in their long red coats,
Canes with a brilliant lacquer shine,
And tall silk hats that were red as wine.
And they pranced with their butterfly partners there,
Coal-black maidens with pearls in their hair,
Knee-skirts trimmed with the jessamine sweet,
And bells on their ankles and little black feet.

[159]

And the couples railed at the chant and the frown
Of the witch-men lean, and laughed them down."

Observing that

> "A good old negro in the slums of the town
> Preached at a sister for her velvet gown,
> Howled at a brother for his low-down ways,
> His prowling, guzzling, sneak-thief days,
> Beat on the Bible till he wore it out
> Starting the jubilee revival shout,"

the poet sees behind this familiar sight a great
day along the Congo when

> "the grey sky opened like a new-rent veil
> And showed the Apostles with their coats of mail.
> In bright white steel they were seated round
> And their fire-eyes watched where the Congo wound.
> And the twelve Apostles, from their thrones on high
> Thrilled all the forest with their heavenly cry:
> "Mumbo-Jumbo will die in the jungle;
> Never again will he hoodoo you."

The anthropology of *The Congo* is hardly to
be trusted. Whatever cults may have existed
among the ancestors of the Afro-Americans, they
themselves are most of them Baptists or Method-
ists, under-educated and under-privileged. Mr.
Lindsay's poem is significant less as a "Study of

the Negro Race" than as an example of a new poetical use to which a certain native material was ready to be put. Here more completely than anywhere else in his work he makes drama out of his reading of life. Is the plight of mankind lamentable in the jungle, among the slums, on the lone prairie? It need not be, as Mr. Lindsay sees it. Somewhere there are crusaders to bring salvation, shouting, singing, beating upon optimistic drums.

4

If Mr. Lindsay's poetry is more original than his philosophy, so is it more valuable. Like all crusaders, he has difficulty in looking ahead to the end of the bright path he follows with such rapture. *The Golden Book of Springfield,* in which he sets forth his notion of what his native town may have become by 2018, is a Utopia of Katzenjammer. History serves him better than prophecy, as when he celebrates the fame of that John Chapman who as Johnny Appleseed is remembered for his gift of orchards to the Middle West. Indeed, Mr. Lindsay is at his best when he is engaged in promoting to poetry some figure or group of figures heretofore neglected by the poets: the Salvation Army, the motorists of the Santa Fe trail, the Springfield blacks, Alexander Campbell, John Chapman, John L. Sullivan, John P. Altgeld, the Bryan of 1896.

On these occasions the poet is not content to write history merely; he makes myths. His Alexander Campbell still rides his circuit, announcing the millennium and snatching back renegade souls to the faith; his John Chapman still roams the great valley, a backwoods St. Francis, with the seeds of civilization in his wallet. During the war, in *Abraham Lincoln Walks at Midnight,* Mr. Lindsay thus poetically brought to life the greatest of all Springfield's citizens, to move restlessly through the streets.

"Yea, when the sick world cries, how can he sleep?"

Poetry, in a conception like this, joins hands with religion, keeping the heroes and the saints and the gods alive because those who depend upon them will not believe that they have died. In a fashion like this patriotism grows up, knitting many hearts together by giving them common memories and common hopes.

And yet Vachel Lindsay is not the personage he was when he published *The Congo* in the same year with *Spoon River Anthology.* Both he and Edgar Lee Masters were deliberately going back to Greek models, the one to the chanted lyric, the other to the ironical epigram. Irony, however, won the day, helped by the presence in the times of a tumult through which nothing less cutting than the voice of irony could reach; and in the eight years since the appearance of the two books the tendency of American literature has been steadily toward irony, satire, criticism. To the drive for the new localism there has succeeded a revolt from the village, turning to ridicule the eloquence of the local patriot and laughing at the manners of the small community. To the confidence that much might be made for literature out of the noisier, rougher elements of the national life by the process of lifting them to richer, surer rhythms and giving them a sounder language, has succeeded the feeling, best voiced by H. L. Mencken, that such elements are menace, nuisance, or nonsense, and that the cause of the higher vaudeville, to be based upon them, is not worth fighting for. Some sense of this shift in the current literary mood must have been responsible, at least in part, for the loss by Mr. Lindsay of the full vigor with which he sang in those first

hopeful days; for his inclination to turn away
from creation to criticism and scholarship, from
poetry to design.

5

The crusader cannot be a connoisseur. He
must meet the masses of men something like half-
way. Nor can it be merely in the matter of
language that he meets them. He must share
as well a fair number of their enthusiasms and
antipathies. He must have gusto, temper, rhetoric; must apply them to topics which are not
too much refined by nice distinctions. These
qualities Mr. Lindsay has, and he lets them range
over a wide area of life, delighting in more things
than his reason could defend. He rejoices, too,
in more things than his imagination can assimi-
late. For Mr. Lindsay's poetical range is not
very great. His eye is bigger than his appetite.
That eye embraces the Anti-Saloon League and
the sons of Roosevelt and Comrade Kerensky and
dozens of such morsels; he gulps them down, but
no digestion follows. He is a reformer, an evangelist. He lifts his standard for all who will
gather round it; he spreads his arms to all who
will come to them. His business is not, as that
of a different poet might be, to find only the pur-

[164]

est gold or the clearest gems. It is rather to spade up new sod and see what unexpected flowers will spring from it; to peer into dusky corners and see that nothing precious has been hidden there; to explore the outer boundaries of the regions of poetry and see if they cannot be extended to include virgin territories hitherto unoccupied. No wonder he has made as many poetic failures as any poet of his rank.

But besides his failures, there are his successes. To appreciate them it is necessary to have heard him read his own verse. His reading is almost singing; it is certainly acting. The rhythms of the camp-meeting, of the cake-walk, of the stump-speech, of the chantey, of the soldiers' march, of patriotic songs, of childish games, throb through him and are from him communicated to the most difficult audience. His singsong is as contagious as that of any revivalist who ever exhorted; his oratory rings. The pulse of human life has beat upon him till he has left its rhythm and meter; simplifying them by his art, he turns and plays with them upon his hearers till they, too, throb in excited unison. Noise by itself, when orderly, has some poetical elements; rhythm, without tune or words, may be thrilling. The potency of Mr. Lindsay's verse, however, shows how far he goes beyond mere noise and rhythm. He has pungent phrases, clinging cadences, dramatic energy, comic thrust, lyric seriousness, tragic intensity. Though he may sprawl and slip and though a large portion of his work is simply sound without importance, he is at bottom both a person and a poet. He is, after all, like no one else. Something in him which was better than his conscious aims has taught him, however much he might borrow from the circuit-rider, the crusader, the booster, that true eloquence comes from the individual, not from the mass; that true poetry is actually lived, not merely shared or argued.

BEYOND GRAMMAR

Ring W. Lardner

IF the freedom of the press is ever destroyed in
the United States, the last barricade to yield
will be the sporting page. The sporting writer
has been allowed to have his fling as long as he
could interest his readers. His fling, however,
has been almost entirely in the direction of novel
language. What he has had to report is news of
a very technical sort, with accurate statistics.
To give variety to his material he has minted
strange coins and carved curious images; he has
done to the common idiom what some gardener
does who makes flowers of amazing color and
scent out of ordinary blossoms. It is true that
the gaudiest flowers of speech, which belong to
the language of base-ball, have of late left the
sporting page of the more civilized newspapers,
which talk less than formerly about "clouting the
sphere" and "kissing the leather" and "carving

the air," because they prefer what is at once plainer and more vivid than these endless twists and turns. But enough of venturesome originality remains in base-ball English (or base-ball American) to make the uninitiated stare and to satisfy the demand among the initiated for a special dialect worthy of the sport. Here is a wide-spread, yet well-knit, guild of players and spectators which has a tradition, a technic, a vogue, a language; no wonder it has also its jongleurs and minstrels in the sporting writers who are read with a delight in their verbal felicities that perhaps no other group of writers in America can be said to waken. Has the guild contributed its share to the sum of literature in the country?

2

Without question it still awaits that genius who in time may lift this particular department of the vernacular to the point to which Mark Twain lifted the department of newspaper humor. Nor does it seem clear how those minstrels and jongleurs, the sporting writers, are to make enduring lays or ballads, sagas or epics, out of news which is dead in a day. The most noteworthy master of the art, Ring W. Lardner, struck off from the highway of the main tradition in *You Know Me Al* and has since gone farther. In that extraordinary document he invented for his protagonist a certain Jack Keefe who is a pitcher expert enough to play with the White Sox and a fool complete enough to tickle even the stupid among the fans by his incomparable stupidity. Jack, babbling with his pen to a friend in his native village, has bragged his way through various base-ball seasons and, in *Treat 'Em Rough* and *The Real Dope,* through his conduct in the war. Both the writer who conceived him and the low-brow public which has received him with noisy joy, have followed his career, apparently, in a mood of relaxation from the hero-worship which too frequently exalts his kind. He imagines he is absolutely indispensable to his team, though his manager often treats him lightly. He imagines every woman he sees is in love with him, though he is a simpleton with women. He imagines he is pugnacious, yet he backs down whenever any one turns upon him; he imagines he is crushing at repartee, yet he makes actually the flattest rejoinders; he imagines he is free-handed, yet he is farcically careful with his money. All the brains he has are in his right arm.

Much as Fenimore Cooper did with Leather-

Stocking, Mr. Lardner has gone beyond his first intentions with Jack Keefe and has exhibited him in numerous situations which call for no change of character but for the continually fresh display of his gifts. Those gifts include a talent for folly and a genius for bad grammar and worse syntax. It is difficult to say whether Jack is better at stumbling into tight places or at explaining himself out of them in a manner which leaves his vanity intact. When he has lost a game, it is always because his team failed to support him as it should have. When a girl turns out not to have been enamoured of him after all, he either argues that there is a broken heart somewhere, not his, or else instantly forgets what he has thought and said about her. He is the dupe of his fellow-soldiers in the war, but he comes home with a foolhardy wound and settles down to be a hero for the rest of his life.

His grammar and syntax, however, are to his folly as genius is to talent. He cuts the knots of language as if there had never been such a thing as a grammarian. Since he is writing, not talking, he permits himself some formalities and he is forced to spell out what in speech he would mumble without much sense of individual words; but he takes the shortest cut he knows how to take between his meaning and his expression. Thus, for instance, he argues the advantages to a soldier of learning French: "But besides that Al after we get to France the French offi~ers will want to tip us off on this and that about the Germans and of course they won't talk to the privates but they will only talk to the officers and if I am a officer by that time which it looks like a cinch I will be one by that time at the outside why suppose I was standing by 1 of our genls. and a French genl. wanted to tell him what was what and etc. but couldn't talk nothing but French and our genl. couldn't make head or tales of it then I could act like an interpreter between the both of them and the first thing you know all the high monkey monks when they want to talk back and forth will be pageing Capt. Keefe or Major Keefe or whatever officer I am by that time." Thus he reports an instance of his wit: "Bodie and Schalk was on [bases] when I come up [to bat] in the 5th and Hill [the opposing pitcher] hollers to me and says I guess this is where I shoot one of them bean balls. I says Go ahead and shoot and if you hit me in the head and I ever find it out I will write and tell your wife what happened to you. You see what I was getting at Al. I was insinuating that if he beaned me with his

[171]

fast one I would not never know nothing about it if somebody did not tell me because his fast one is not fast enough to hurt nobody even if it should hit them in the head. So I says to him Go ahead and shoot and if you hit me in the head and I ever find it out I will write and tell your wife what happened to you. See, Al? Of course you could not hire me to write to Violet but I did not mean that part of it in earnest."

Thus he deftly arranges for a truce between his wife and Al: "Now old pal I know that Florrie hasn't never warmed up toward you and Bertha and wouldn't never go down to Bedford with me and pay you a visit and every time I ever give her a hint that I would like to have you and Bertha come up and see us she always had some excuse that she was going to be busy or this and that and of course I knew she was trying to alibi herself and the truth was she always felt like Bertha and her wouldn't have nothing in common you might say because Florrie has always been a swell dresser and cared a whole lot about how she looked and some way she felt like Bertha wouldn't feel comfortable around where she was at and maybe she was right but we can forget all that now Al and I can say one thing Al she never said nothing reflecting on you yourself in any way because I wouldn't of stood for it but instead of that when I showed her that picture of you and Bertha in your wedding suit she made the remark that you looked like one of the honest homely kind of people that their friends could always depend on them." Jack is the comic mirror of American illiteracy.

He is more than a mirror of illiteracy; he is a treasure-trove. In Jack's maundering confidences Mr. Lardner has assembled countless examples of murdered English caught by one of the most accurate ears now occupied with the vernacular. Malapropisms, misspellings and mispronunciations, paradigms simplified and distorted by ignorance, incredible triumphs over syntax—these appear in such numbers that a treatise could be based upon them. But they are woven into a pattern and fitted to a character with a skill which few mere philologists have ever had. Though Mr. Lardner has preferred to drop to a plane of speech which is lower than most native humorists have studied, and has had consequently to do the hard work of bringing the idiom into a kind of uniformity so that it could be written down, he has not lost himself altogether in linguistic tricks. He knows the customary behavior of his illiterates as well as he

knows their tongue. He has comic force which
could have made him a humorist in any dialect.

3

So far he has kept close to his original formula no less with his later characters than with
Jack. Both *Gullible's Travels* and *The Big
Town* continue the American tradition of humorous autobiography, delivered in each of these two
cases by an amusing illiterate who strays into
unfamiliar paths and tells about them in his vernacular. The narrator of one goes to the opera,
tries a season at Palm Beach, learns to play
bridge; the narrator of the other visits New York
to have a taste of life in hotels, in furnished
apartments, in suburban resorts, at the races, at
the theaters. The fun is largely verbal, but back
of such frivolities lie facts of character not to be
overlooked. The men whom Mr. Lardner uses
as his spokesmen represent a type which is strik-
ingly American. Although, as traders or as
sportsmen, they have seen the world, they have
seen it altogether with their bodily eyes. They
read nothing but the newspapers or some accidental book, and that solely for entertainment.
They are as innocent of reflection as of culture.

When they have dreams, they are of the simplest, most sentimental kind: of inheriting an easy fortune, of telling a captious boss to go to hell, of seeing a son become President. They are wholly at the mercy of their wives, who, thanks to labor-saving devices and small families, have leisure to dabble in superficial accomplishments or to think of climbing into a society more conspicuous than their own. In *Gullible's Travels* and *The Big Town* most of the adventures occur while the characters are having a mild, unsuccessful fling in snobdom.

The creator and chronicler of Babbitt, with whom all of Mr. Lardner's principal characters would feel immediately at home, approached his theme in a passion for the beauty and the intelligence which he saw that the Babbitts, by their very nature, miss. Mr. Lardner, in his books at least, gives no sign of any æsthetic or intellectual concern. He laughs at affectation; he is jovial toward foolishness; he portrays dullness without anger. His instinct for the facts of life and for the comedy of facts is too strong for him to feel obliged to bring his more serious reading of existence into his accounts. As his hard-boiled heroes take their look at the world, uninfected by its novelty or by its complexity, he forgets how thick-skinned they are, because they tickle him so much by their self-reliance. The narrator in *The Big Town* is a provincial Mid-Westerner who nevertheless feels as much at home in New York as Benjamin Franklin felt in Paris or Mark Twain in Jerusalem. Much of what would embarrass or appall a more reflective man does not touch this knowing Hoosier at all. He is that perennially popular figure in American fiction, the Yankee unabashed. The things which do impinge upon his consciousness he takes in very quickly and turns to his own idiom. And how glib he is! He speaks the special jargons of business and of sport and of poker, beside his own loose but competent lingo. His invention never flags, as his nerve never weakens. Wherever he is, there is no opportunity for languor, for hesitation. He and his wife and her sister are as vulgar as suspenders, but they are set forth with such verve that their story has a force quite separate from its power to satirize or edify. Here, as in all Mr. Lardner's books, there is effected a masterly translation of American life into the vernacular of the low-brows. Are there in that life such things as wonder, splendor, distinction, criticism, enlightenment?

Yes, but how do they look when seen through low-brow eyes, when reduced to the common denominator of the mass of men?

4

That Mr. Lardner, despite his gifts, is still essentially a comic philologist, appears from his lack of variety in all but language. He has only two characters: one is Jack, bragging about his prowess in love and war (including base-ball); and the other is a case-hardened low-brow, under whatever name, seeing the world with his slightly snobbish wife. With this second character Mr. Lardner has even used one plot repeatedly, ringing minor changes upon a scheme to get the wife's sister married to some reluctant suitor. In *Gullible's Travels* this is the theme of two out of the five stories; in *The Big Town* it is the theme or sub-theme of all of them. Always the husband is bored by the sister or positively dislikes her; always the wife gives herself without a touch of humor to the earnest pursuit; always the sister, coy but undeterred, accepts the rôle of matrimonial bait, no matter what the discomforts of the hook or the disinclination of the victim. Only the victim varies. And he is essentially the same always, being or pretending to be the kind

[177]

of fairy prince the eager sisters would like to catch—prosperous, generous, cheap. Whatever is made of such matters must be made within the narrow limits of a formula.

These stories, read as rapidly as they follow one another in a book, not with weeks or months between them as in a magazine, suggest a form of popular art which in the newspapers ordinarily stands close to the sporting page. That is the comic strip, wherein a set of personages of established and unchanging characteristics daily meet with mishaps for the amusement of the populace. There friends are forever falling out, husbands are forever bullied by their wives, parents are forever fooled or corrected by their children, snobs are forever being snubbed, dreamers are forever waking up. It is one of the most skeptical, most cynical, most heartless universes ever invented. No person in it modifies his actions or his language to spare another's feelings. One strip is entirely devoted to the outbursts of a violent hero who does to bores and nuisances what all men would like to do but cannot do in a reasonably civil community. In something of this fashion, though with words, not fists, the husband of Mr. Lardner's formula expresses himself to his family and friends. In real life such remarks as his would rankle for years, but in these stories they leave no scars. So with the predatory maiden of the formula, who, if she were real, would perish of mortification during her long defeat, but who instead comes up smiling after each unhappy skirmish and returns to the chase. All of Mr. Lardner's characters have the short memories of the persons of the comic strip, as they have their lack of personal dignity, undisturbed by the figure they cut when buffeted or tumbled about. And this is because, like the characters of farce, they give the impression of living in space but not in time. In the world of reality and of realistic art the people who live there are forever growing, becoming. They cannot stand still, like puppets ready to be dressed up for any plot or like weather-vanes revolving with whatever wind may blow. It is Mr. Lardner's failure to perceive this, or to act upon the perception if he has it, that excludes him from the rank to which his capacities should admit him. He has created convincing characters; he has put convincing words into their mouths; he has set them going in a convincing dance of life. But there he has stopped, too often content to

[179]

play old tricks until the action seems mechanical and his audience wonders whether his characters are convincing, after all. He has still to rid himself of the ephemeral qualities both of the sporting page and of the comic strip.

DAY IN AND DAY OUT

Manhattan Wits

THE editorials in American newspapers were once personal affairs. They were made by hand and their readers knew whose hand it was that had fashioned this or that comment upon the news of the morning or evening. Now, however, personality has given way to something less diversified. A newspaper is known by the policy it keeps. As a rule the special editorial hand is not to be recognized except by experts, whose guesses, moreover, are occasionally wrong. But personality is too obstinate a thing to be easily expelled. Thrown out through the door, it comes back through the window and is shortly as much at home as ever. The generation in America which saw the distinctive color dying out of editorials saw at the same time the rise of the distinctive paragraph which kept the editorial section from settling down to any monotony of sense. Deft paragraphers multiplied and made their papers famous. Publisher strove with publisher to catch and develop writers who could be themselves and be amusing every day. Out of so much imitation, so much competition, a standard form emerged. Eugene Field set the standard, as regards dimensions, at a column, and went a long way toward setting the standard as regards themes and methods. He poked fun at current folly, he told jokes on himself, he turned out yards of brisk, bright verses in his column called "Flats and Sharps." Field lived, however, to divide his honors with George Ade, also a columnist in Chicago, who in his "Stories of the Streets and Towns" at once specialized and broadened the functions of their sort of humor. Since Field died and Mr. Ade gave up his column, few decided novelists have been introduced among the paragraphers. Bert Leston Taylor with his "A Line o' Type or Two" long carried on the tradition in Chicago. Other cities have their local wits, several of them of amazing fecundity and pungency. But in New York, to which so many things are drawn by its sheer magnitude, the column has at present its greatest prestige and influence.

There the successful members of the guild en-

joy reputations which are unequaled by those of
any other contemporary authors. They have, of
course, advantages, Not perhaps monthly, like
story-writers, nor perhaps annually, like novelists or dramatists, but daily they appear before
their publics; and their publics daily number
hundreds of thousands of readers in New York,
with possible millions elsewhere for those of the
columnists who are taken up by newspaper syn-
dicates. Appearing thus punctually, these wits
can pounce first upon the news and make, or pub-
lish, the earliest *mots* on topics that invite them.
Appearing thus regularly, these same wits, having beat up their game, can chase it with comic
persistence as long as need or interest lasts. Being so topical, they are naturally for the most
part also local. They retail the gossip, promul-
gate the jests, discuss the personalities, represent
the manners of New York. To read them in any
distant city is to miss half the points they make,
or at least half the freshness of their points.
They are licensed jesters of the town, free to
catch the most respectable citizen momentarily
off his guard, without fear of being taken too
seriously. They can turn a mayor to ridicule,
send hundreds to a theater or keep dozens away
from it, stimulate the sales of a book, give a

clever phrase household currency, fix public attention upon some neglected figure or episode, past or present, laugh some general hysteria to sleep.

The great audiences which they have by virtue of their positions they hold by their particular qualities. They are immensely personal. They take the public into their confidences with whimsical candor. One of them devotes a day each week to publishing his diary. Another calls out joyfully when he has found a new book or a new drink. Another humorously records his progress in getting rid of superfluous pounds of flesh. Another makes charming capital out of the sayings and doings of his son. Thus through the confusion of the daily news they pick their ways and yet preserve their identities. Readers who have found events more or less impartially reported and more or less judicially discussed, like still to find them touched with the hand of comedy by a definite person. The columnists are a perpetual relief from what may be called the newspaper grand style. Nothing is too great for them to bring it before the bar of laughter; nothing is too small for them to flash a beam of light upon it. It is true that they are sometimes accused of forming a smug corporation, exchanging compliments from column to column, overpraising one another's books and plays, capriciously shutting out the dull barbarians who do not habitually cross their paths; but these accusations have so far not become very ominous. If the columnists were not felt to be untrammeled personalities, they would not be felt at all.

There are, indeed, more than four of such Manhattan wits who have each a loyal following. The four, however, who are most widely known and followed happen among them to cover virtually all the ground that the columnists ever cover. They are, as no one questions, Franklin P. Adams of "The Conning Tower," Christopher Morley lately of "The Bowling Green," Don Marquis of "The Lantern," and Heywood Broun of "It Seems to Me."

2

Mr. Adams is in a strict sense the wit of the group. He is the neatest of them all with his gay verses, the crispest of all with his puns. He has a satirical taste for exact language. He catches up instances of bad grammar, of loose diction, of mixed metaphor, wherever he comes upon them, and exposes them in his column. He dislikes what is hackneyed no less than what is inexact.

To give a kind of dramatic emphasis to his quest for platitudes he invented Dulcy and then put into her mouth all the threadbare phrases and sentiments which tickled or irritated him. Much interested in words and facts, he is less interested in large ideas, large speculations. He is quick to dissent from general statements and to weaken them by pointing out exceptions. Eloquence does not melt him nor cosmic melancholy subdue him. He walks as stubbornly along the broad way of common sense as Horace did. He has a feeling for the classics which has led him, like Eugene Field, to make numerous Horatian versions and parodies. He has a delight in first-hand documents which has led him to adopt the manner of Pepys in his weekly record of adventures around town. Yet both in his Horatian and in his Pepysian modes, Mr. Adams is contemporary and vernacular. He brings his masters down to date. He seems quick and hard and sure, a man never to be found napping, the very quintessence of Manhattan.

Because of his cautious habits he limits himself to a relatively narrow range of theme. Very many of his witticisms are merely verbal; many of them are very trivial and some of them are cheap. He concerns himself, on the whole, rather with the foolish things men say than with the foolish things they do. He seldom touches public affairs more closely than to point out some misquotation or solecism in a speech by some public man. The taste for gossip grows upon him. Something kindred in his constitution turned him to Pepys. At the same time, Mr. Adams is more than a gossip. There is that pungency of comment, not too savage and not too easy-going, with which he falls upon absurdities and affectations. He has much that is Horatian in his constitution too, so much that it has been contagious and has bred a whole school of Horatian imitators. He draws to his column, and publishes in it, the most edged, the most stinging, the most impudent annotations upon the minor occurrences of the day. He is almost infallible in rejoinder. It is perhaps his dexterity and insouciance, his gyroscopic balance, which have seemed to his followers to be his most delightful traits; yet there must not be overlooked that touch of plaintiveness which adds a special interest to his charm. Again and again he lets slip some hint of the despair he feels when he encounters supreme loveliness in poetry and by it measures his own jaunty product. Back of that alert self-possession of his lies a certain engaging modesty which his followers sense without realizing. Like the dyer's hand, he is stained by the materials he works in. At heart, however, he is primarily a poet who has been taught by the nice technic of his art to be a wit as well.

3

Mr. Morley is as expansive as Mr. Adams is self-possessed. His manner is all mellowness. Nothing about him, if he can help it, betrays the fact that he is the youngest of these four columnists. Seasoned in Oxford, he has the air of a man who has been reading old books and drinking old wine with old friends before a fire of old wood. His muse has haunted many libraries and has brought back many antiquarian treasures. At his pen's end he has the vocabulary of the Elizabethans, the idioms of the seventeenth century. A great deal of fine liquor, apparently, has flowed under his bridges. He knows where the best food may be obtained and ransacks ancient volumes for imaginary meats. He is a connoisseur of tobacco and understands to a nicety the conduct of a pipe. He talks spaciously of pets and children; his most considerable book has a hero who may be taken for either a dog or a man. Mr. Morley has a robust feeling for life lived out of doors and a special taste for the sea and ships. Into all these subjects of discourse, his port of entry is likely to be a literary one. What he writes is full of echoes; he abounds in parodies; he can fit himself to obsolete modes of verse or prose with marked facility. It is to be suspected that Dickens helped him to like ale and that Joseph Conrad helped him to like oceans. But there is nothing pedantic about Mr. Morley's tastes. His special quality is the heartiness with which he takes his public into his confidence on all the topics that enlist him. He has shown many persons who did not guess it before, what magic there is in dingy shops filled with dusty books. He has dug up curious authors, such as Sir Kenelm Digby, out of an obscurity which might have been expected to be immortal. He has considerably enriched the imagination of his followers by laying a new stress upon the pleasures of eating and drinking, of playing and laughing, of collecting good things and living jovially among them, of preferring scholarship to jazz.

He encourages enjoyment rather than reflection. When he touches upon speculative themes he touches, as a rule, only the most general ones. He is a liberal whose liberalism comes from spontaneous sympathies, without too much analysis. His comments upon the passing show rarely bite and never pulverize. He is bland and lacks the concentration of sardonic wits. Mellowness, it has been suggested, came over him before he was ready for it. When did he serve his years in the conscript army of rebellion which human life perennially raises among its youth? To the more ironical among his readers, there seems something unknit and ungirt about his persistent gusto. Yet it must be seen that what he lacks in point he partly makes up in energy. Not only his daily column but books as well pour from him in a broad stream. And it must be seen, too, that he has traveled a long way from the adolescent lushness of his juvenilia. His sinews have tightened, his style has grown firmer, his observations have taken on a deeper tone. No one can quite prognosticate his course. Moods of adventure and fresh ardors are plainly stirring in him. If his column, and all the columns, were to be wiped out tomorrow by some solemn dictatorship, Mr. Morley would fall upon his feet and would find that he could walk alone in any one of several paths, most successfully in the path of poetry or of the whimsical novel. Meanwhile he keeps a kind of literary inn, invit-

ing all who are not too austere or too sophisticated
or too serious to take their ease with him in a
taproom filled with congenial smoke in which numerous pleasant fellows endlessly and convivially
discuss affairs of taste and exchange agreeable
scandal about the universe.

4

What distinguishes Mr. Marquis from his
rivals among the columnists is a racy substance
in him which makes him able to create character
as no one of the others can. He has more point
than Mr. Morley; he has a more burly energy
than Mr. Adams; but he lives for his public
primarily in the careers of those preposterous,
fascinating personages who wander on and off
his daily stage. That they are in outline the
broadest kind of caricature does not seem to matter. Archy the cockroach, Mehitabel the cat,
Hermione the platitudinarian, Fothergil Finch
the minor poet, Prudence Hecklebury the incomparable prude, Captain Fitzurse the swaggerer,
Al the bartender, the Old Soak who in dry days
lifts his thirsty voice with incredible ingenuity of
protest—they all have their absurd outlines filled
in with comically real human elements. Mr.
Marquis has the gift of using a vernacular tech-

nic with classical materials. Once he has hit upon a given character, he continues to exploit it almost as if he were a cartoonist with a set figure to show off day by day in slightly new adventures. Archy must forever give his messages to the world by jumping from the ceiling to the keys of a typewriter and so pounding out his insect observations; Mehitabel must be true to her motto: *"Toujours gai*—What the hell!"; Miss Hecklebury each night before retiring must roll her peach under the bed to see that no dangerous male is there; Hermione must keep up her brainless babble to prove that she keeps up with every silly fad; the Old Soak must see the whole universe through a softening haze of alcohol. Yet these obvious devices are only tricks employed to catch running readers who might be surprised to learn at how many points Archy and Mehitabel suggest the beast fables of medieval France and how often Captain Fitzurse suggests the braggart soldier of Latin comedy. There is of course no imitation to be hinted at. The likenesses come from the fact that Mr. Marquis fixes his eyes upon the aspects of the comic scene which in every age attract shrewd satirists. And he is more than a mere satirist, winging folly in his own person. He is so much of a dramatist that

he must invent stalking-horses behind which to
shoot and must make the creatures look so much
alive that they seem at any moment about to gal-
lop off on their own affairs.

Having in him the substantial quality needed
by a creator of characters, Mr. Marquis seems
something more, also, than a mere town wit. He
suffers less than most of the New York columnists when put to the test of being read at a distance from New York, possibly because he has
spent a larger part of his life outside metropolitan circles. He knows provincial humors and
turns of speech. Without being in any respect
a small-town philosopher, he has a knack at understanding and reproducing the processes of
thought and the shades of feeling which belong
to villages rather than to cities. In this sense he
smacks of the American soil as it exists in the in-
terior districts which cosmopolitan humorists find
chiefly laughable. If his methods suggest the
cartoonist of the comic strip, so do they suggest
the older tradition of native humor as it descends
from Jack Downing and David Crockett to
Artemus Ward and Mark Twain. He is robust,
hilarious, given to vast exaggeration, capable of
vituperative outbursts. Even when he appears
simply wrong-headed, as in his sentimental

praise of booziness, he conducts his arguments with such random vitality that they are funny. The same vitality marks his verse, which ranges from graceful lyricism to a mad mélange of topsy-turvy burlesque. In verse as in prose he moves with a rush that carries him frequently through his whole column with a single item, which he may find it necessary to continue to another day. It is significant, however, that he loses something when he turns to the conventional forms of literature: his stories are not particularly distinguished, and the successful play which he built around the Old Soak has little besides its leading character to recommend it. Mr. Marquis is thus proof that, no matter how many elements may enter into the art of the columnist, it is a special art, requiring certain special gifts no one of which in the case of any individual columnist can by him be safely dispensed with.

5

How varied columnists can be appears from the fact that Mr. Broun writes for the same page of the same newspaper as Mr. Adams and that neither ever extinguishes or often dims the other. So far as Mr. Broun is concerned this would be the fact no matter by whose side he might do his daily turn. His method is outwardly very simple. He writes no verse, he throws no verbal handsprings, he invents no personages for his column. He talks about himself and his opinions. As he is not bothered by false reticences and as his mind never stops revolving, his topics are singularly numerous. Whether he talks about religion, politics, economics, sex, sport, books, plays, or personalities, he says what he thinks with the same candor and the same ease. He has this advantage over others of his guild, that he is also a dramatic critic and the best all-round sporting writer of his time, and is so prolific as to spill the flood of his disquisition beyond the borders of his own paper into many others. But though he thus attracts an unusual amount of attention to himself, he does it by his abundance rather than by any common egotism. He illustrates the paradox that if a writer is only personal enough he achieves impersonality as well. There is, after all, something very impersonal about the free mind. Though Mr. Broun does actually color all his discourse with his own unmistakable qualities, his aim is to simplify and to elucidate. There is no harm done if he simplifies and elucidates on his own terms; if, for instance, he dislikes books unless the characters behave as he himself approves, whatever the art of the narrative, and if he insists upon reasonable codes of human conduct which do not always allow for as much perverse complexity as human nature insists upon displaying in difficult moments. Mr. Broun makes perfectly clear what his terms are and then proceeds with a humane logic which it is virtually impossible to refute without recourse to arguments which are likely by comparison with his to sound like prejudices.

He stands in the long line of American commentators, from Franklin through E. W. Howe, who have sharpened their wits upon contemporary topics and have thereby made their names remarkable. But whereas most of them have been prudential and conservative, Mr. Broun is steadfastly provocative and radical, at least as regards ideas. If he is not eminently hospitable to novel methods of expression, this is because he is not eminently interested in them. He writes in the simplest way himself and does not greatly care to dig and to pry for meanings in other writers. Directness of mind and manner is his forte; his distinction arises from the zest with which he hunts new ideas and from the skill with which he puts them to work upon raw materials. He must have many readers who, having come to this or that hasty judgment upon some contemporary topic, discover that Mr. Broun's thinking begins where theirs left off. Unlike the majority of sensible men, who give the impression that they are leading the discussion back to first principles, Mr. Broun gives the impression that he is leading it forward to them. He lifts common sense to that plane on which it is enlightenment. Without doubt it is his good fortune to have flourished in an age when enlightenment is a literary fashion, when conservatism, however powerful, is extraordinarily dull. His prosperity, however, depends less upon his luck than upon his ability to bring a fresh, honest mind to all sorts of current themes. In this he is assisted by his loyalty to newspapers for their own sake. Though he has written novels and has collected some of his sketches within formal covers, he does not give the impression, in his column, of hoarding his words for more permanent refuge elsewhere. Often loose, often diluted, he keeps up an intelligent fire, not too much worried about a future for his arrows if only he can bring down his daily game.

6

The race of columnists, however, are not in too important a degree shaped by the race of newspapers which are their medium. They are town wits, as Addison and Steele were in their merry London, as Irving and Paulding were in the New York of a hundred years ago. Like their elder prototypes, the columnists occasionally foregather in what might once have been called taverns or coffee houses, or sit each in his favorite haunts with his friends and hangers-on. The things they say, it happens, do not now have to be caught up and spread by the gossip of the listeners. There are the daily columns yawning to be filled with light, gay, personal by-products of such conversations. To the little periodicals in which Addison and Steele, Irving and Paulding published their essays, and which were as sounding-boards to convey their voices beyond their immediate circles, have succeeded the metropolitan newspapers in which the columnists appear, and which may more properly be compared to radio instruments designed to broadcast them over a good part of the continent. The difference in the audiences makes, of course, differences between the periodical essayists and the columnists. And yet by virtue of their essential qualities these column conductors, closely as they fit their times, continue a tradition which goes back to one of the earliest moments in the history of human fun—the moment when cities began to demand of their wits a more edged, more sophisticated, more varied, and more continuous entertainment than had been demanded among the farms and villages.

III. POSTSCRIPT

THE FRIENDLY ENEMY

Carl Van Doren

WITHOUT being clever or notably astute, Carl Van Doren has always been lucky. Ten years ago, when he set out to become a specialist in American literature, he seemed to many of his friends to be cutting off his future with an ignorant if not with a deliberate knife, much as if he were some improvident youth who had vowed, against all advice, to court Cinderella while she still huddled among her cinders. Then came the sudden prosperity of Cinderella. New poets began to step forth on every bough and sing; new novelists discovered that honesty is a good policy in their trade; new critics lifted powerful and not entirely untrained voices which were heard in circles heretofore quite innocent of such exciting sounds; even new dramatists wriggled in the womb of eternity. Commentators and interpreters being called for, Mr. Van Doren became one of them. The call was, not improbably, something of a surprise to him. His first considerable task had been the translation of a German play; his first book had been the biography of an English wit and scholar who led his biographer through whole libraries of Greek, with epicyclic visits among Latin and Italian, French and Spanish authors. Moreover, in his recent specialism Mr. Van Doren had been less a critic than a minute historian, working dustily with editorial spade and plow to pile up the mountain of monographs known as *The Cambridge History of American Literature*. Out of that he was happily permitted to salvage and enlarge certain chapters and to call them *The American Novel*. Had he been still solely a professor he would doubtless have ended his narrative with 1900, perhaps with a curt epilogue upon the newer novelists. But having been invited, by his greatest stroke of luck, to be an editor of *The Nation*, that home of good causes and upholder of good literature, he snatched the opportunity to combine his duty to his history with his duty to his journal. *Contemporary American Novelists* was the consequence and established Mr. Van Doren in such reputation as he has. There remained for him only to collect various of his opuscula in *The*

THE FRIENDLY ENEMY

Roving Critic, and, having gone to a new field in *The Century Magazine,* to look about for other contemporaries to study in his latest volume, *Many Minds.*

It may be hoped that there is some connection between his sense that he has been rather fortunate than deserving and his discreet methods in criticism. So far as it is possible for a critic, he stands quietly, if not stealthily, behind his work. The shortest of the pronouns is almost the rarest of the words he uses; if he were writing about himself, he would be likely to write in the third person. Whatever noise he makes in the world he prefers to make vicariously, with the subjects of his criticism the real protagonists— his subjects, in fact, and not his victims. They are, as he sees the matter, the source and end and test of the critic art. The authors who mean enough to warrant criticism do not always reveal their meanings unmistakably. Their books have been conceived in passion and brought forth in enthusiasm, these at one period of growth and those at another, some successfully and some unsuccessfully. Public opinion concerning any given author is generally confused, based upon loose hearsay, false guesses, insufficient knowledge of his whole significance. To the problem thus arising Mr. Van Doren likes best to address himself. Intending to exercise no craft but that of sympathy, he turns the documents of his author over and over until he has found what he believes to be the central pattern. This is his chief delight in criticism: to find a pattern where none has been found before. He would probably stop here if he had his choice, but being by profession a journalist, and having so many pages to fill each week or month, he goes on to his explanation of the pattern and his incidental interpretation of the author to the general public. His business with the problem ends, he thinks, when he has made it clear to the limit of his capacity. He leaves to other-minded critics the fun of habitually pointing out what meanings, what patterns, would be better.

Confined as he has been by his specialism to the literature of one country during barely three centuries, and still further confined, for the most part, by his journalism to writers of the present century, Mr. Van Doren nevertheless surveys his field not without perspective. Euripides is the tragic dramatist, Lucretius the poet, Montaigne the essayist, Fielding the novelist, Heine the wit, Shaw the comic dramatist, Socrates and Leonardo da Vinci the persons, and the saga-writers the historians whom this home-keeping specialist and punctual journalist actually most enjoys. Yet in his criticism he seldom ventures into argument by comparison. With what must seem a kind of chameleon ardor he has managed to discuss the most varied types of Americans: Edwards and Paine, Cooper and Theodore Dreiser, George Ade and George Santayana, Mark Twain and Henry James, Melville and Marion Crawford, Howells and Stephen Crane, Whitman and Robert Frost, James Branch Cabell and Vachel Lindsay, E. W. Howe and Upton Sinclair, Stuart P. Sherman and H. L. Mencken, Edith Wharton and Edna St. Vincent Millay. A striking number of these subjects of his analysis, and those not the least diverse in aims and achievements, testify that Mr. Van Doren has come as close to their designs as any critic can decently be expected to come. He would, however, be one of the promptest to admit, what he has had enough critics to point out, that he is singularly, if not fatally, non-committal. Where are the scalps, they ask him, that should dangle bloodily at the critic's belt? Is so much impartial interpretation anything but virtually so much praise? Has the roving critic no preju-

dices, no principles, no causes? Is he a critic
of many minds and therefore a man of none at
all?

2

In answering these questions it is only just to
turn the tables upon so reserved a critic and to
look for any pattern, any ground-plan, which
may underlie his movements. What first of all
appears is his preference for those authors who are
civilized: intelligent, skeptical, ironical, lucid.
Viewing the general life of mankind, its dim history, its shifting manners, its tangled aspirations,
as a thing which is, for the artist, both raw materials and fair game, Mr. Van Doren looks particularly in an author for the mind, the rational
conception of existence, by which he shapes his
matter. This may be a mind as detached and
disciplined as George Santayana's, as impetuous
and loose as Vachel Lindsay's, as speculative as
Mary Austin's, as empirical as George Ade's, and
Mr. Van Doren can still give it all the benefit of
the philosophic doubt whether one kind of mind
is absolutely better than another; but he does not
really sympathize with it unless it stands def-
initely on the side of the reason as against superstition or mere tradition. That prejudice of his

appears even in his discussion of such harmless ephemerides as the local colorists of the last century: "They scrutinized their world at the instigation of benevolence rather than at that of intelligence; they felt it with friendship rather than with passion." It appears, too, in his attitude toward such a technical matter as plot. "Mr. Wells . . . lacks the sort of creative imagination which can follow a great theme to a great conclusion. For this, what is needed is essentially a great character." By a great character Mr. Van Doren means, as in this passage does not quite appear, an ardent loyalty to a reasoned ideal, persisting to its ultimate conclusions. On the whole he is more insistent upon the reasonableness of the ideal than upon the ardor of the loyalty. He does not greatly trust impetuous surmises or mystical illuminations: "Civilization, after all, is but the substitution for first thoughts of second or third or hundredth thoughts, reason supplanting passion, and polity guiding anarchic instinct"; "All the tools with which mankind works upon its fate are dull, but the sharpest among them is the reason"; "At least as much good is done in the world by the devils who merely question as by the angels who merely pray; and the devils are more entertaining."

So implicit a confidence in the rational faculties
of the human race might well suggest in Mr. Van
Doren an exaggerated taste for the universal, the
abstract, the mathematical, or the smart in literature were it not offset by his equally implicit
confidence in an element which he discusses in
connection with his favorite doctrine of "the
fourth dimension in criticism." It is not enough,
he argues, to ask about a masterpiece only "Is
it good?" "Is it true?" "Is it beautiful?"
There is still the unavoidable query "Is it alive?"
"The case of Socrates illustrates the whole argument. Was he good? There was so great a
difference on this point among the critics of his
time that the majority of them, translating their
conclusions into action, put him to death as dangerous to the state. Was what he taught the
truth? . . . It seems clear that he had his share
of unscientific notions and individual prejudices
and mistaken doctrines. Was he beautiful? He
confused Greek orthodoxy by being so uncomely
and yet so great. But whatever his shortcomings
in these regards, no one ever doubted that he was
alive—alive in body and mind and character,
alive in war and peace and friendship, alive in
bed and at table. Life was concentrated in him;
life spoke out of him. So with literature, which

collects, transmutes, and utters life. It may represent the good, may speak the truth, may use the modes of beauty—any one or all of these things. Call the good the bow which lends the power; call the truth the string which fixes the direction; call the beautiful the arrow which wings and stings. But there is still the arm in which the true life of the process lies. Or to change the figure, one of those gods who in the mythologies model men out of clay may have good clay and a true purpose and may shape his figure beautifully; but there is still the indispensable task of breathing the breath of life into it before it will wake and go its own course and continue its breed to other generations. Life is obviously what makes the difference between human sculpture and divine creation; it is the same element which makes the difference between good literature and dead literature. . . . Neither creator nor critic can make himself universal by barely taking thought about it. He *is* what he *lives*. The measure of the creator is the amount of life he puts into his work. The measure of the critic is the amount of life he finds there."

Mr. Van Doren is of course aware that this creed of vitality can not be held to equip the

critic with any idiot-proof formula for estimating
works of art. Not all persons will agree upon
what it is that makes a book alive, and some will
find a book throbbing when others find it cold.
No scheme of measurement is impartial or precise
enough to determine whether Shakspere creat-
ing Hamlet or Goethe appreciating the achievement was indubitably more or less alive than
the random citizen cracking his best joke or his
companions roaring at it. Criticism, however,
being rarely the concern of random citizens, finds
it prudent to consider the processes of the Shaks-
peres and Goethes whom it does concern. Thus
biased to the side of experts, the critic habitually
tends to lose himself in technical considerations,
to admire masterpieces because of the minor difficulties they have overcome, to approve the exquisite adjustments of matter to form. By this
tendency the pedants and puritans of criticism
are manufactured. To resist it the critic who
wishes to be alive must keep his attention fixed
much of the time upon the primary substances
of art: the stormy passions of mankind, the
swarming hopes, the noisy laughter, the homely
speech. Let him be delighted as he may be by
the final product, he must still, behind all the

modes of literature except those whose chief merit
is their artifice, feel the rough document. He
must understand that the best civilized poets or
novelists, though perhaps not the most civilized,
have shaped their art out of materials which, being original and obstinate, did not too glibly slip
into neat molds. For Mr. Van Doren it has
doubtless been easier to be a critic of this sort
than it might have been had he worked with some
literature not so relatively rich in documents as
the literature of America and not so relatively
poor in final products. But his chosen specialism
has exacted a penalty. It has confirmed him in
his native disposition to overlook deficiency in
art for the sake of abundance of vitality. Back
and forth over the continent of American literature, with possibly too much gusto and certainly
not enough fastidiousness, he has moved in search
of biographers, travelers, amateur anthropolo-
gists, adventurers, and eccentrics no less than of
conscious artists; and he has expounded them all
with a sympathy which is to blame if now and
then the swans and geese, the sheep and goats,
within Mr. Van Doren's critical fold look un-
warrantably of the same dimensions and significance.

[213]

3

Taken in some candid moment, this friendly critic would undoubtedly admit that sympathy, however valuable a function of criticism, is not its total function.   There are authors who deserve less to be explained than to be attacked like weeds in a useful or lovely garden, without too much consideration for their unavoidable instinct to be weeds.   But for such lethal functions Mr. Van Doren has apparently small appetite.   He has, with all his considerable industry when enthusiastic, the particular kind of indolence which seeks to avoid controversy.   Though his vivisection of Booth Tarkington and of Winston Churchill seems to have been accomplished with certain cruel thrusts and twists of the scalpel, he ordinarily prefers to use in such cases the colder knife of silence.   Nor is this preference the result of any calculated pride, unwilling to stoop to the smaller fry of letters.   It comes from a positive aversion to reading undistinguished or trifling authors and to doing the hard work upon them which goes into Mr. Van Doren's criticism.   If he touches an author of this sort at all, it is because he thinks the author's works have settled into a false place in history. Rather an historian, strictly speaking, than a critic, Mr. Van Doren is bold enough where history is in question. He has labored untiringly to dig the weeds out of the annals of American fiction; he was nearly the first to lift a voice in the revival of Herman Melville; among his contemporaries he reaches a probably too eager hand to many if not to all kinds of excellence, in something the spirit of a radical historian quick to welcome new materials to the record. Being so occupied with history, that is, with things already done, Mr. Van Doren has almost no interest in the metaphysics of criticism. He seldom struggles in the speculative void where subtler critics argue about the boundaries and purposes of art. He undertakes only plain jobs with definite materials. He sets forth the patterns which he believes he has found in his subjects of investigation as if they were any other contribution to knowledge. Subtler critics may disagree with him, but he does not return to the theme unless he has found new facts which force him to modify his opinions. Though no longer given so much as formerly to minute research, he still insists that his usefulness, if he has any, must be based upon the opportunity which he affords for unprofessional readers, with his professional help, to make up their own minds about the authors whom he interprets.

The truth of the matter is, Mr. Van Doren practises one branch of criticism to the exclusion of several others. That he is little perturbed by his limitations, that he does not greatly care to rise to passion or to descend to prejudice, means, in part, that he is more wilful in his behavior than sometimes appears. It means, also, that criticism has never been with him a major aim. What really interests him is human character, whether met in books or out of them, and it is always human character which he studies. His fourth volume of more or less formal criticism being now completed, he plans, so far as it may be permitted him, to withdraw to other provinces.

BIBLIOGRAPHIES

BIBLIOGRAPHIES

MARY AUSTIN

The Land of Little Rain. Boston, 1903.

The Basket Woman: Fanciful Tales for Children. Boston, 1904.

Isidro. Boston, 1905.

The Flock. Boston, 1906.

Santa Lucia. New York, 1908.

Lost Borders. Boston, 1909.

Outland. By Gordon Stairs [pseudonym]. London, 1910. As by Mary Austin, New York, 1919.

The Arrow-Maker: A Drama in Three Acts. Produced, New York, 1911; published, New York, 1911. Revised edition, Boston, 1915.

Christ in Italy: Being the Adventures of a Maverick among Masterpieces. New York, 1912.

A Woman of Genius. Garden City, 1912. Revised edition, Boston, 1917.

The Lovely Lady. Garden City, 1913.

The Green Bough: A Tale of the Resurrection. Garden City, 1913.

Fire: A Drama in Three Acts. Produced, Carmel, California, 1914; published in The Play Book, Madison, October–December, 1914.

California: The Land of the Sun. New York, 1914.

Love and the Soul-Maker. New York, 1914.

BIBLIOGRAPHIES

The Man Jesus: Being a Brief Account of the Life and Teaching of the Prophet of Nazareth. New York, 1915.

What the Mexican Conference Really Means. New York, 1915. (Pamphlet)

The Man Who Didn't Believe in Christmas. Produced, New York, 1916.

The Ford. Boston, 1917.

The Young Woman Citizen. New York, 1918.

The Trail Book. New York, 1918.

No. 26 Jayne Street. Boston, 1920.

The American Rhythm. New York, 1923.

Contributor to: The California Earthquake of 1906. Edited by David Starr Jordan. San Francisco, 1907; The Sturdy Oak: A Composite Novel of American Politics by Fourteen American Authors. . . . Theme by Mary Austin. New York, 1917; The Path on the Rainbow: An Anthology of Songs and Chants from the Indians of North America. Edited by George W. Cronyn. New York, 1918; The Cambridge History of American Literature, Volume IV. New York, 1921.

GEORGE ADE

Artie: A Story of the Streets and Town. Chicago, 1896. Dramatic version, produced, New York, 1910.

Pink Marsh: A Story of the Streets and Town. Chicago, 1897.

Doc Horne: A Story of the Streets and Town. Chicago, 1899.

Fables in Slang. Chicago, 1899.

BIBLIOGRAPHIES

More Fables. Chicago, 1900.

Forty Modern Fables. New York, 1901.

The Girl Proposition: A Bunch of He and She Fables. New York, 1902.

The Sultan of Sulu. Produced, Chicago, 1902; published, New York, 1903.

People You Know. New York, 1903.

Clarence Allen. Phoenix, 1903.

Handsome Cyril. Phoenix, 1903.

In Babel: Stories of Chicago. New York, 1903.

Circus Day. Akron, 1903.

Peggy from Paris. Produced, Chicago, 1903.

The County Chairman. Produced, New York, 1903.

Rollo Johnson. Phoenix, 1904.

Breaking into Society. New York, 1904.

True Bills. New York, 1904.

The College Widow. Produced, New York, 1904.

The Sho-Gun. Produced, New York, 1904. (With Gustav Luders)

The Bad Samaritan. Produced, New York, 1905.

Just Out of College. Produced, New York, 1905.

In Pastures New. New York, 1906.

Marse Covington. Produced, New York, 1906; published, Washington, 1918.

The Slim Princess. Indianapolis, 1907.

Father and the Boys. Produced, New York, 1908.

Mrs. Peckham's Carouse. Produced, New York, 1908.

The Fair Co-Ed. Produced, New York, 1909. (With Gustav Luders)

The Old Town. Produced, New York, 1910. (With Gustav Luders)

BIBLIOGRAPHIES

I Knew Him When—: A Hoosier Fable Dealing with the Happy Days of Away Back Yonder. Chicago, 1910.

Hoosier Hand Book. Chicago, 1911.

Knocking the Neighbors. New York, 1912.

Speaking to Father. Produced, New York, 1913.

Ade's Fables. New York, 1914.

Nettie. Produced, New York, 1914.

Hand-Made Fables. New York, 1920.

Single Blessedness and Other Observations. New York, 1922.

E. W. HOWE

The Story of a Country Town. Atchison, 1883. Boston, 1884.

The Mystery of the Locks. Boston, 1885.

A Moonlight Boy. Boston, 1886.

A Man Story. Boston, 1889.

An Ante-Mortem Statement. Atchison, 1891.

The Confession of John Whitlock, Late Preacher of the Gospel. Atchison, 1891.

Lay Sermons.

Paris and the Exposition.

Daily Notes of a Trip Around the World. Topeka, 1907. 2 vols.

The Trip to the West Indies. Topeka, 1910.

Country Town Sayings: A Collection of Paragraphs from the Atchison Globe. Topeka, 1911.

Travel Letters from New Zealand, Australia and Africa. Topeka, 1913.

The Hundred Stories of a Country Town.

BIBLIOGRAPHIES

Preaching of a Poor Pagan.
Success Easier than Failure. Topeka, 1917.
The Blessing of Business. Topeka, 1918.
Ventures in Common Sense. New York, 1919.
The Anthology of Another Town. New York, 1920.

ROBERT FROST

A Boy's Will. London, 1913. New York, 1915.
North of Boston. London, 1914. New York, 1915.
Mountain Interval. New York, 1916.
Selected Poems. London and New York, 1923.
New Hampshire: A Poem with Notes and Grace Notes.
    New York, 1923.

   Contributor to: A Miscellany of American Poetry
       1920. New York, 1920; American Poetry 1922:
       A Miscellany. New York, 1922.

STUART P. SHERMAN

Porro Unum Est Necessarium: or The Gaiety of Soc-
    rates. Urbana, Illinois, 1915. (Pamphlet)
Matthew Arnold: How to Know Him. Indianapolis,
    1917.
On Contemporary Literature. New York, 1917.
American and Allied Ideals: An Appeal to Those Who
    Are Neither Hot Nor Cold. Washington, 1918.
Americans. New York, 1922.
The Significance of Sinclair Lewis. New York, 1922.
    (Pamphlet)
The Genius of America: Studies in Behalf of the
    Younger Generation. New York, 1923.

[223]

BIBLIOGRAPHIES

Editor: Treasure Island by Robert Louis Stevenson. New York, 1911; Coriolanus by William Shakespeare. New York, 1912; A Book of Short Stories. New York, 1914; 'Tis Pity She's a Whore and The Broken Heart by John Ford. Boston, 1915; Essays and Poems by Emerson. New York, 1921; The Poetical Works of Joaquin Miller. New York, 1923.

Associate Editor: The Cambridge History of American Literature. New York, 1917–1921. 4 vols.; A Short History of American Literature. New York, 1922.

Introductions to: John Fordes Dramatische Werke. In Neudruck herausgegeben von W. Bang. Erster Band. Louvain, Leipzig, London, 1908; The Scarlet Letter by Nathaniel Hawthorne. New York, 1919; The George Sand-Gustave Flaubert Letters. Translated by Aimee L. McKenzie. New York, 1921; Leaves of Grass by Walt Whitman. New York, 1922; American Prose Masters by W. C. Brownell. New York, 1923.

George Santayana

Sonnets and Other Verses. Cambridge, 1894.

The Sense of Beauty: Being the Outlines of Aesthetic Theory. New York, 1896.

Lucifer: A Theological Tragedy. Chicago, 1899.

Interpretations of Poetry and Religion. New York, 1900.

A Hermit of Carmel and Other Poems. New York, 1901.

The Life of Reason or The Phases of Human Progress. New York, 1905. 5 vols. Second edition with a new preface, New York, 1922.

BIBLIOGRAPHIES

Three Philosophical Poets: Lucretius, Dante, and Goethe. Cambridge, 1910.

Winds of Doctrine. London, 1913.

Egotism in German Philosophy. London, 1915. Translated into French, Paris, 1917.

Philosophical Opinion in America. London, 1918. (A lecture)

Character and Opinion in the United States with Reminiscences of William James and Josiah Royce and Academic Life in America. London, 1920.

Little Essays Drawn from the Writings of George Santayana by Logan Pearsall Smith with the Collaboration of the Author. London, 1920.

Soliloquies in England and Later Soliloquies. London, 1922.

Poems . . . Selected by the Author and Revised. New York, 1923.

Scepticism and Animal Faith: Introduction to a System of Philosophy. London, 1923.

The Unknowable. Oxford, 1923. (A lecture)

Contributor to: Essays in Critical Realism. London, 1920.

EDNA ST. VINCENT MILLAY

Renascence and Other Poems. New York, 1917.

Aria da Capo: A Play in One Act. London, 1920. New York, 1921.

A Few Figs from Thistles: Poems and Four Sonnets. New York, 1921. Enlarged edition, New York, 1921.

[225]

BIBLIOGRAPHIES

Second April. New York, 1921.

Two Slatterns and a King: A Moral Interlude. Cincinnati, 1921.

The Lamp and the Bell: A Drama in Four Acts. New York, 1921.

The Ballad of the Harp-Weaver. New York, 1922.

The Harp-Weaver and Other Poems. New York, 1923.

Contributor to: American Poetry 1922: A Miscellany. New York, 1922.

H. L. MENCKEN

Ventures into Verse: Being Various Ballads, Ballades, Rondeaux, Triolets, Songs, Quatrains, Odes and Roundels, All Rescued from the Potters' Field of Old Files and Here Given Decent Burial [Peace to Their Ashes]. New York, 1903.

George Bernard Shaw: His Plays. Boston, 1905.

The Philosophy of Friedrich Nietzsche. Boston, 1908. Revised edition, Boston, 1913.

Man *versus* The Man: A Correspondence Between Robert Rives La Monte, Socialist and H. L. Mencken, Individualist. New York, 1910.

The Artist: A Drama Without Words. Boston, 1912.

Europe after 8:15. New York, 1914. (With George Jean Nathan and Willard Huntington Wright)

A Book of Burlesques. New York, 1916.

A Little Book in C Major. New York, 1916.

A Book of Prefaces. New York, 1917.

In Defence of Women. New York, 1918. Revised edition, New York, 1922. Translated into German, Munich, 1923.

[226]

BIBLIOGRAPHIES

Damn: A Book of Calumny. New York, 1918. Reissued as: A Book of Calumny, New York, 1919.

The American Language: A Preliminary Inquiry into the Development of English in the United States. New York, 1919. Revised editions, New York, 1921, 1923.

Prejudices: First Series. New York, 1919.

Heliogabalus: A Buffoonery in Three Acts. New York, 1920. Translated into German, Berlin, 1922. (With George Jean Nathan)

Prejudices: Second Series. New York, 1920.

The American Credo: A Contribution toward the Interpretation of the National Mind. New York, 1920. Revised edition, New York, 1922. (With George Jean Nathan)

The Literary Capital of the United States. Chicago, 1920. (Pamphlet)

Prejudices: Third Series. New York, 1922.

Spiritual Autopsies. Boston, 1922. (Pamphlet)

A Personal Word. Boston, 1922. (Pamphlet)

Editor: The Players' Ibsen. Boston, 1909 (2 vols.: A Doll's House, Little Eyolf); The Gist of Nietzsche. Boston, 1910; Blanchette and The Escape by Eugène Brieux. Boston, 1913; The Free Lance Books. New York, 1919—(6 vols. to date: Youth and Egolatry by Pio Baroja; Ventures in Common Sense by E. W. Howe; The Antichrist by Friedrich Nietzsche; We Moderns by Edwin Muir; Democracy and the Will to Power by James N. Wood; In Defence of Women by H. L. Mencken).

BIBLIOGRAPHIES

Contributor to: The Borzoi 1920. New York, 1920; On American Books. Edited by Francis Hackett. New York, 1920; Civilization in the United States. Edited by Harold Stearns. New York, 1922; These United States: A Symposium. Edited by Ernest Gruening. New York, 1923–1924. 2 vols.

Introductions to: The Master Builder, Pillars of Society, Hedda Gabler by Henrik Ibsen. New York, 1918; The House of Pomegranates and The Nightingale and the Rose by Oscar Wilde. New York, 1918; Tales of Mean Streets by Arthur Morrison. New York, 1920; The Line of Love by James Branch Cabell. New York, 1921; The Nietzsche-Wagner Correspondence. Edited by Elizabeth Foerster-Nietzsche. New York, 1921.

Pistols for Two. By Owen Hatteras. New York, 1917. (Biographical notes on George Jean Nathan and H. L. Mencken, by some authorities conjectured to be autobiographical)

CARL SANDBURG

Incidentals. Galesburg, 1907. (Pamphlet)
Chicago Poems. New York, 1915.
Cornhuskers. New York, 1918.
The Chicago Race Riots, July, 1919. New York, 1919.
Smoke and Steel. New York, 1920.
Rootabaga Stories. New York, 1922.
Slabs of the Sunburnt West. New York, 1922.
Rootabaga Pigeons. New York, 1923.

BIBLIOGRAPHIES

Contributor to: A Miscellany of American Poetry
1920. New York, 1920; American Poetry 1922:
A Miscellany. New York, 1922.

VACHEL LINDSAY

The Tree of Laughing Bells. New York, 1905. (Pamphlet)

The Last Song of Lucifer. New York, 1908. (Pamphlet)

God Help Us to Be Brave. New York, 1908. (Pamphlet)

The Tramp's Excuse and Other Poems. Springfield, Illinois, 1909. (Pamphlet)

The Village Magazine. Springfield, 1910. A second number, Springfield, 1920.

Rhymes to Be Traded for Bread. Springfield, 1912. (Pamphlet)

General William Booth Enters into Heaven and Other Poems. New York, 1913.

Adventures While Preaching the Gospel of Beauty. New York, 1914.

The Congo and Other Poems. New York, 1915.

The Art of the Moving Picture. New York, 1915. Revised edition, New York, 1922.

A Handy Guide for Beggars Especially Those of the Poetic Fraternity: Being Sundry Explorations, Made While Afoot and Penniless in Florida, Georgia, North Carolina, Tennessee, Kentucky, New Jersey, and Pennsylvania. . . . New York, 1916.

The Chinese Nightingale and Other Poems. New York, 1917.

BIBLIOGRAPHIES

The Golden Whales of California and Other Rhymes in The American Language. New York, 1920.

The Daniel Jazz and Other Poems. London, 1920.

The Golden Book of Springfield. . . . : Being the Review of a Book That Will Appear in the Autumn of the Year 2018, and an Extended Description of Springfield, Illinois, in That Year. New York, 1920.

I Know All This When Gipsy Fiddles Cry. San Francisco, 1922.

Going-to-the-Sun. New York, 1923.

Collected Poems. New York, 1923.

RING W. LARDNER

Bib Ballads. Chicago, 1915.

You Know Me Al: A Busher's Letters. New York, 1916.

Gullible's Travels, Etc. Indianapolis, 1917.

Treat 'Em Rough: Letters from Jack the Kaiser Killer. Indianapolis, 1918.

My Four Weeks in France. Indianapolis, 1918.

The Real Dope. Indianapolis, 1919.

Own Your Own Home. Indianapolis, 1919.

Regular Fellows I Have Met . . . with Illustrations by Regular Cartoonists. Chicago, 1919.

The Young Immigrunts. By Ring W. Lardner, Jr., with a Preface by the Father. Indianapolis, 1920.

Symptoms of Being 35. Indianapolis, 1921.

The Big Town: How I and the Mrs. Go to New York to See Life and Get Katie a Husband. Indianapolis, 1921.

BIBLIOGRAPHIES

The Follies of 1922. Produced, New York, 1922.
(With Victor Herbert and others)

The 49ers. Produced, New York, 1922. (With Franklin P. Adams, Heywood Broun, and others)

Say It with Oil: A Few Remarks about Wives. New York, 1923. (In the same volume, Say It with Bricks; A Few Remarks about Husbands, by Nina Wilcox Putnam)

Compiler: March 6th. The Home Coming of Chas. A. Comiskey, John J. McGraw, James J. Callahan. Compiled by Ring W. Lardner and E. G. Heeman. Chicago, 1919.

FRANKLIN P. ADAMS

In Cupid's Court. Evanston, Illinois, 1902.

Lo. Produced, Milwaukee, 1909. (With O. Henry)

Tobogganing on Parnassus. Garden City, 1911.

In Other Words. Garden City, 1912.

By and Large. Garden City, 1914.

Weights and Measures. New York, 1917.

Among Us Mortals. Boston, 1917. (Text to drawings by W. E. Hill)

Something Else Again. New York, 1920.

Overset. Garden City, 1922.

Women I'm Not Married To. Garden City, 1922. (In the same volume, Men I'm Not Married To, by Dorothy Parker)

The 49ers. Produced, New York, 1922. (With Ring W. Lardner, Heywood Broun, and others)

So There! Garden City, 1923.

BIBLIOGRAPHIES

CHRISTOPHER MORLEY

The Eighth Sin. Oxford, 1912.

Parnassus on Wheels. Garden City, 1917.

Songs for a Little House. New York, 1917.

Shandygaff: A Number of Agreeable Inquirendoes upon Life and Letters, Interspersed with Short Stories and Skits. . . . Garden City, 1918.

The Rocking Horse. New York, 1919.

The Haunted Bookshop. Garden City, 1919.

In the Sweet Dry and Dry. New York, 1919. (With Bart Haley)

Mince Pie: Adventures on the Sunny Side of Grub Street. New York, 1919.

Three's a Crowd. Produced, New York, 1919. (With Earl Derr Biggers)

Travels in Philadelphia. Philadelphia, 1920.

Kathleen. Garden City, 1920.

Pipefuls. Garden City, 1920.

Hide and Seek. New York, 1920.

Tales from a Rolltop Desk. Garden City, 1921.

Plum Pudding, of Divers Ingredients, Discreetly Blended and Seasoned. Garden City, 1921.

Chimney Smoke. New York, 1921.

Where the Blue Begins. Garden City, 1922.

Thursday Evening. Cincinnati, 1922.

Translations from the Chinese. New York, 1922.

The Story of Ginger Cubes. New York, 1922.

Rehearsal: A Comedy in One Act. Boston, 1922. (In: A Treasury of Plays for Women. Edited by Frank Shay)

[232]

BIBLIOGRAPHIES

The Powder of Sympathy. Garden City, 1923.

Inward Ho! Garden City, 1923.

Parsons' Pleasure. New York, 1923.

Editor: Modern Essays. New York, 1921.

Introductions to: Explorers of the Dawn by Mazo de la Roche. New York, 1922; Parodies on Walt Whitman. New York, 1922.

DON MARQUIS

Danny's Own Story. Garden City, 1912.

Dreams and Dust: Poems. New York, 1915.

The Cruise of the Jasper B. New York, 1918.

Hermione and Her Little Group of Serious Thinkers. New York, 1918.

Prefaces. New York, 1919.

The Old Soak and Hail and Farewell. Garden City, 1921. Dramatic version of The Old Soak produced, New York, 1922.

Carter and Other People. New York, 1921.

Noah an' Jonah an' Cap'n John Smith: A Book of Humorous Verse. New York, 1921.

Poems and Portraits. Garden City, 1922.

Sonnets to a Red-Haired Lady (by a Gentleman with a Blue Beard) and Famous Love Affairs. Garden City, 1922.

The Revolt of the Oyster. Garden City, 1922.

HEYWOOD BROUN

The A. E. F.: With General Pershing and the American Forces. New York, 1918.

BIBLIOGRAPHIES

Our Army at the Front. New York, 1918.

Seeing Things at Night. New York, 1921.

Pieces of Hate and Other Enthusiasms. New York, 1922.

The Boy Grew Older. New York, 1922.

The 49ers. Produced, New York, 1922. (With Ring
W. Lardner, Franklin P. Adams, and others)

The Sun Field. New York, 1923.

> Contributor to: Nonsenseorship: . . . Sundry Ob-
> servations Concerning Prohibitions, Inhibitions
> and Illegalities. Edited by George Palmer Put-
> man. New York, 1922.

CARL VAN DOREN

The Life of Thomas Love Peacock. London, 1911.

The American Novel. New York, 1921.

Contemporary American Novelists 1900–1920. New
York, 1922.

The Roving Critic. New York, 1923.

Prudence Militant. Atchison, 1923. (Pamphlet)

Many Minds. New York, 1924.

> Translator: Judith: A Tragedy in Five Acts. By
> Friedrich Hebbel. Boston, 1914.
> Contributor to: Shaksperian Studies by Members of
> the Department of English and Comparative Litera-
> ture in Columbia University. New York, 1916.
> Managing Editor: The Cambridge History of Ameri-
> can Literature. New York, 1917–1921. 4 vols.;
> A Short History of American Literature. New
> York, 1922; The Modern Student's Library:
> American Division. New York, 1922—(4 vols.

[234]

to date: Leaves of Grass by Walt Whitman. With an Introduction by Stuart P. Sherman; American Ballads and Songs. Collected and Edited by Louise Pound; The Autobiography of David Crockett. With an Introduction by Hamlin Garland; American Prose Masters by W. C. Brownell. With an Introduction by Stuart P. Sherman)

Editor: Tales by Washington Irving. London, 1917; Benjamin Franklin and Jonathan Edwards: Selections from Their Writings. New York, 1920; Seven Stories by Nathaniel Hawthorne. New York, 1920; Tales by Nathaniel Hawthorne. London, 1921; Selections from the Writings of Thomas Paine. New York, 1922; Moll Flanders by Daniel Defoe. New York, 1923; White Jacket by Herman Melville. London, 1924.

Contributing Editor: The Masterpiece Library of Short Stories. Edited by William Robertson Nicoll, A. T. Quiller-Couch, George Saintsbury, and others. London, 1920. 20 vols.

INDEX

INDEX

INDEX

[239]

INDEX

INDEX

INDEX